Contemplating Lent:

40 days of Spiritual Practice leading up to Easter

CONTENTS

FORWARD

One of the events that set me on this contemplative path was the opportunity to attend spiritual retreat several years ago. I had just begun to wander out of my evangelical Christian roots. My assumption about a weekend away was that it would be filled with "worship" music, sermons, and instructions around what actions were correct and incorrect in my everyday life.

This retreat came at things from quite a different perspective.

I spent the weekend in ritual, meditation, silence, and fasting. These were no evangelicals. They had tapped into something primal. Later, the person who had helped the whole trip happen for me asked what I thought.

I was filled with a dizzying array of emotions. I was overwhelmed, thankful, surprised, raw. I said, "I came here expecting to play with sparklers. And you people? You lit me on fire."

This strikes me as an apt description of the gulf between where the church is on Easter, and where it should be. We have settled for playing with sparklers. The process is meant to set us on fire.

There are, of course, a variety of downsides to being lit on fire. Not to put too fine a point on it, but the prospect of being lit on fire is terrifying. There is no logical way to defend such a course of action: no words that might be said to make this seem like a good idea.

But aren't you just a little bit intrigued? If you are anything like me, there is something primal about the idea of symbolically setting the self on fire. I suspect St. John of the Cross might have been thinking this way when he declared that he was a candle.

Perhaps the mystic was on to something. A candle is something that is made to be set on fire. In this strange identity claim, he is, perhaps, implying that we too are made to be set on fire. Based on my experiences at the strange and powerful retreat, I would like to offer my own resounding, "Yes! Yes, we were made to be set on fire."

The intention of this book is to help return Easter and the 40 days before it to its rightful, incendiary position in our lives.

Many smart and well-intentioned people have attempted to express this fire in words. We put so much importance on doctrine, sermons, books, lists, and rules. Trying to describe fire to someone who is cold, and who never saw flames before would be foolish. Words don't warm and descriptions fall short. Most of the time this has resulted in squabbling and *us vs them* dualistic boundaries. As best as I can, I am going to try and avoid this debate in these pages. This is not a book of doctrine. Of course, as a book, it is comprised of words. But the words are not the point. It is not about a specific idea, an end result, a product. It is about a process; the act of doing the practices and considering where these take you.

There are two things I hope you will experience as you read this book.

The first is a deepened experience of the forty days preceding Easter. This is a powerful corner of the Christian calendar. Like anything powerful, it has the potential to be misunderstood... even abused. Many of us have wrestled with the meaning of Jesus' death. This time can be characterized by guilt as difficult explanations are offered. Weighty theological understandings are not bad things. But they are also not enough.

It will be my goal in these pages to sidestep doctrine and disputes. There are plenty of places you can find these if you are looking for them. Whatever abstract ideas we have are greatly enhanced by personal experience. For centuries, Christians have engaged in a wide variety of spiritual practices, perhaps more at Lent than any other time of the year. Contemporary Christianity has largely turned its back on these practices, much to its detriment.

In short, my first hope for readers is that they will experience the Easter season in a new way. I hope that this experience will be powerful and productive.

My second hope is that this might be an opportunity for you to deepen your spiritual practice. My own life has been immeasurably improved by cultivating a routine of meditation, prayer, and contemplative activities. Forty days of trying these practices out is not a bad thing. But Forty weeks? Or Forty years? That (and there is lots of science available to back this claim up) will change everything.

In other words: my hope for you is that you will carry some of these practices forward. I have arranged this book to focus on five specific practices. These will be explained in greater details next chapter. It might be that not all five of these practices resonate with you. Perhaps you will only continue your practice of one of these types of practice, or two. Whichever you choose, I know that they will offer you up great gifts.

INTRODUCTION

There are many types of spiritual practice. Perhaps there are just as many ways to categorize these practices. I have a hope to deepen the experience of Lent for you. But I would also like this to be a convenient springboard into continuing these practices beyond this season. For this reason, it seemed wise to organize this book in a way that lead to some reflection about the various types of spiritual practices that are out there. Please know that the groupings I landed on are not complete or perfect. They are a good place to start, though.

The spiritual practices in this book are arranged into sections of five practices. Each grouping begins with a sacred reading practice, moves into a breath prayer, a visualization, a mind-clearing exercise, and an apophatic meditation. Because Lent consists of 40 days, this book is arranged into 8 of these 5-day groupings. It is not expected that a reader has any experience with any of these practices before beginning.

There has been a tension at work within me as I wrote this book. I think it's good to name that tension here.

On the one hand Lent is a time that we are focused on the following of Christ. Precisely what it means to follow Christ varies wildly, of course. I am sure that my preconceptions and areas of ignorance have colored my experience and representations of what this looks like. But I have done my best to be respectful of the various Christian traditions as I have written this book.

On the other hand, I am increasingly convinced that an interspiritual orientation has so much to offer us. There is a rich, sometimes suppressed history of uniquely Christian contemplation. Nonetheless, we are so lucky to be alive at this time, when gifts from other religious traditions are so easy to come by. Many of the practices in this book have been colored by the perspectives and practices of non-Christian traditions. A few, such as the riverside meditations, originated completely in other religions. I hope that my usage of these practices here is respectful and honors their original spirit.

Just as this book is neither the time nor place for a discussion of what it is the crucifixion meant, it is also not a treatise on the ways that Christianity should interface with the other great spiritual traditions in the world. My increasing comfort with borrowing from the gifts of other traditions is not rooted in the sort of doctrine that can be expressed in words. It begins with the increasing conviction, as I devote myself to spiritual practice, that I am doing the same sort of thing as brothers and sisters who are contemplatives within their own traditions. I do not believe we will ever wash away the differences between our paths. I do not see a time where it is irrelevant to describe myself as a *Christ-centered* mystic. But I know that I am both a brother to those who follow Christ and to those who identify as mystics, regardless of their orientation.

Let's return to the more practical matters at hand. It is difficult to express a precise amount of time that ought to be devoted to these practices each day. Rather than expressing where I think you ought to begin, I would suggest that you make a goal of getting yourself to 30 minutes a day by the end of this forty-day period.

If thirty minutes sounds terrifying to you, hang in there. We don't have to jump straight to 30 minutes tomorrow. I would recommend that your first days of practice are just a little bit outside of your comfort zone. If it feels like five minutes would be easy, commit to yourself something just a bit beyond the easy. Perhaps, for the first ten days, you will practice each day for 8 minutes.

When you get to days 11-20, you might shoot for fifteen minutes each day. On days 21-30, perhaps 25 minutes each day is your goal. And for those last ten days, perhaps devote an entire 30 minutes to your practice.

The specific duration of time you choose is less important than your ability to stick to your plan. In other words, it would be better to decide that you will spend ten minutes a day on your practice and complete this time than to plan to do thirty minutes each day and only complete twelve.

I am going to let you in on a little secret to help explain why it is so important to stick to your goal in this area:

Spiritual practices? They aren't always fun. They are good, they are worth it. But if this was easy, we wouldn't need to read books about them to make them stick.

One of the reasons that they are not fun is that most of us are not particularly good at sitting. There are lots of reasons why we have created these noisy, busy lives. One of the most profound reasons for the noisiness and the busyness of our lives is that many of us are uncomfortable with the silence.

We are uncomfortable with silence because silence is the place where we meet the things that we are afraid of. Quiet is the place where we face the things we fear. At some point, we began to run from the sadness, despair, and loneliness. When it is too quiet, we began to think about that thing we should not have said. When we have this down time, we begin to feel these feelings we wish we didn't feel. None of this is easy.

Filling up our schedules until they are about to burst? That is easy. Turning on the radio all the time? We don't even need to reach down between the seats anymore. Automakers put the controls right there on the steering wheel now.

The problem is that once we start running, it is very difficult to stop. One of the greatest gifts of the contemplative's stance is that she discovers something that she might have known intellectually. But for the first time, we experience this up close and personal: *None of these things can harm us.*

The image I return to, again and again, is that all these fears are a bit like a small yippee dog. One of those annoying ones with delusions of toughness. It sits behind a fence and barks away at the trucks that pass by every single day. If a person removed the fence the dog would likely chase the trucks for a period of time. But what would the dog do if the truck stopped?

Our fears and worries and concerns are like that little dog. Our personhood, our soul, our very self is that giant truck. The dog makes lots of noise. It cannot hurt us. But we only discover this when we stop.

Things will come up during your time of meditation. There will be days that it feels like you have barely done the practice at all. This thought or that keeps coming up. The natural response is to see these as the days you were not successful. That is not accurate. Those might have been some of the best days for your spiritual growth.

But the growth only really happens when we face these things down. When we push ourselves a little further than we had planned. The natural tendency is to engage a practice until it feels uncomfortable. So, if we made the unrealistic goal to keep going for thirty minutes, we will stop it when we get here, to minute number twelve. When things started to get uncomfortable. When the growth was just about to happen. It is true, of course, that if we had only set the goal of sitting for ten minutes, we might not have gotten to this uncomfortable spot either. Our time might have been up before we got there.

But if we set a goal of ten minutes and we make it ten minutes; we have set an important foundation. We have begun to train the metaphorical annoying dog. He does not run the show here. His barking will not alter the program. We are going to sit as long as we plan to sit, and he can bark to his little doggie heart's content. We are going to continue to do the things we set out to do.

It is important that the above considerations are held in balance with an even more important reality: it is very important that we do not overdo this. Please practice good self-care. Living outside your comfort zone is very good. Placing yourself in distress is not.

Please seek out the love and support of your network or mental health professionals when you need it. Some of us--

including your author-- have experienced a reduction in the amount of professional mental health support we required after we began to take spiritual practices seriously. Not everyone will experience this. Therapy and medications are very important. Spiritual practice might enhance the effectiveness of these interventions. Despite all this, there is something very important to be said here. Lots of damage has been done by people who have ignorantly proclaimed that therapy and medications are unnecessary for a person who has a "right" relationship with God.

Therapy and medications are gifts from God. They have changed the lives of many. Whether the medication is for depression or type II diabetes, whether the therapy is for a knee injury or a broken heart, those of us who can access these to make our lives better should access these to make our lives better.

In addition to committing to a certain length of time each day, there are a few other things you can do to enhance the effectiveness of your practice. Contemplative practices might best be experienced in community. If you have a friend, partner, or group that can do these practices together that is likely to be very powerful. Even if meeting each day is not feasible, knowing that others are doing these each day and planning to meet once each week to discuss them is a great thing.

Even if you will be doing them alone, setting a specific time and place to do these practices each day is also highly recommended. I notice that this does more than just increase the possibility of follow through. When I make these practices into a sort-of ritual they take on a different ambiance. Even the preparation becomes an act of meditation or even worship. If I always do my practice first thing in the morning, the act of waking up begins to feel like a part of my spiritual practice. If I always meditate in the recliner next to my bed, the simple act of positioning the chair I always use begins to feel like a part of the practice itself.

The next eight chapters of this book are groups of five spiritual practices. Each of these groupings is lain out identically. Each will be a bit of a microcosm for the Lenten journey itself.

We begin in light and understanding, belief in the power of words. Within each grouping, we will slowly travel out of this light and ease into darkness and mystery. Darkness is not bad or evil. It is unknown, of course. And scary as a result. On some scale, each of these five days can be seen like it begins with a loud and boisterous entry into Jerusalem. There is a sense of victory and familiarity. But we slowly travel down a road that leads to mysterious and unprecedented death and resurrection.

As you begin this book there is no assumption being made that you will be familiar with these practices. Thorough instructions will be given on each day. For now, let's take a brisk run through each of them.

Each chapter, we begin with sacred reading practices. This helps to set the stage for the meaning of these forty days. Lent is a strange time. On the one hand, it is a rather direct walk to Jesus' death and resurrection. On the other, it has been a historical consideration of Jesus' time in the desert. The sacred reading section reviews the accounts of both of these.

The second day in each chapter is a breath prayer. Breath prayers are light and airy things. They are easy and accessible. Moving into these practices feels like an accurate representation of the first days in the desert when Jesus was strong and sure. It is also evoking the surety that he and his followers might have carried when they were farthest from the cross.

On the third day, we take on a visualization. We fill the imagination with an image or narrative that helps us to see this time in a new way. Here, we begin to step away from the known and scripted.

The second-to-last day in each grouping is one which helps us to empty the mind and release intrusive thoughts. Here, we accept the world as it is, seeking to remove our projections and assumptions about what is happening.

Things begin to grow dark. The time in the desert drags on. The cross begins to loom. The final exercise in each grouping will be an apophatic meditation. Apophatic meditation is a powerful approach to facing the difficulties of life in a non-dualistic manner.

It might be observed at this time that one of the practices most commonly associated with Lent has not yet made in an appearance in these pages. Lent is quite closely connected to the practice of fasting. In my experience, it can be powerful. It can also be difficult, and unhealthy. The topic of fasting probably deserves an entire book on its own. I have shared a few observations about this topic in the appendix. If you are thinking about some sort of fast through Lent perhaps you will find it helpful to jump to that section at the end of this book. There are many possibilities available to us with out even considering a fast though. I believe that your season can be complete with out one, let's begin then, with our first grouping of practices to take us through these first five days of the season.

THE FIRST GROUPING:
DAYS 1-5

Recall that most of this book will be structured into 5-day sections. Each of these sections will begin with a sacred reading practice. The second day of each grouping will feature a breath prayer. The third day of each grouping will feature a visualization. The fourth day will feature an exercise focused on emptying the mind. The fifth day will focus on an apophatic meditation.

In today's introductory section, I would like to spend a few minutes making some last-minute suggestions for getting the most out of this book.

I don't know about you, but I am pretty good at making the things happen that I want to. I might tell you and even myself that I really tried to do these other things. But somehow, the things I really wanted to do in the first place are the things I end up making happen. When I really want to make something happen, I make a plan for it to occur. I know how to get there. I have considered obstacles and have considered how to overcome them. I remember to do all the things I need to do in order to make this thing a reality.

If there is a movie coming out this weekend that I really want to see, I will probably check the times a day or two before. I will communicate with the people I want to see it with. I will consider in advance if there is anything else going on at that time. If I want to see a movie, I will have handled all the silly little details that stand in my way.

On the other hand, I am not particularly good at getting to the doctor. When I know that I need to make an appointment I will have a vague idea that at some point I need to call. I won't give much forethought to how and when to make that call. If something pops up that makes it difficult to do that, I won't exhibit much creativity in getting around these obstacles. If it is difficult to get to the appointment, I won't think twice about calling to cancel. I am learning that I create a bit of a win-win for myself when I don't plan very effectively. I can tell myself that I tried. I can simultaneously avoid the doctor.

It's pretty silly, when you start to compare the relative benefits of seeing a movie with going to the doctor.

I know lots of people who plan to cultivate a spiritual practice. The problem is that they plan to meditate in the same way that I plan to go to the doctor. They have a vague plan to do it at some point. They have not pondered the obstacles. They won't exhibit much flexibility if something interferes with this poorly defined plan.

The people who actually start meditating are the people who have the approach I have to seeing a movie this weekend. It is not easy to take this approach. There are ways in which spiritual practices are, in fact, a bit more like going to the doctor than they are like going to a movie. It can feel like something we should do, rather than something we want to do. And so, we resist it.

The reality is that mostly, we do things we want to do. Mostly we don't do the things we don't want to do. Sometimes the unexpected occurs and gets in our way. But more often than not we use the things that happen to cover up and justify the decisions we were going to make all along.

I also understand that most changes are part of a process. It might be that a plan to begin spiritual practices through this Lent is part of your process. Perhaps it will not stick this time around. If you got through three days last time you tried to meditate, and you get through six days this time, you are well on your way. Perhaps you will try again in a year, and at that point you will make this a part of your routine for a whole month.

I am sure that mostly we do the things we wanted to do

in the first place. I am also sure that beating ourselves up for being human does not change this fact about ourselves. So, wherever you are in this process, and whatever change these practices make, I wish you peace on this journey.

DAY 1: SACRED READING PRACTICE

Background: Over these 40 days, we will look at several different passages of the bible. Traditionally, Lent explores both Jesus' 40 days in the desert and the time of his crucifixion and resurrection. We will explore these events here, too.

The specific sacred reading practices we will use fall into two general categories. The first is *Lectio Divina.* The second sacred reading practice is sometimes called Holy Imagining. Each of these two practices has a wide variety of variations. Though we will re-use some of the passages of scripture from one grouping to another, each practice will be unique in that we will be trying a different version of *Lectio* or Holy reading.

Over these next several weeks we will take a deeper look into the definitions and implementation of these practices. Let's begin, today, with a broad pair of descriptions: *Lectio Divina* is a general category of prayerful reading techniques. Generally speaking, these processes is broken into a time of reading, meditate, pray, and contemplate. The details of what these four activities mean is best experienced within the context of actually doing it.

Holy Imagining is a process of using the senses to place ourselves within the events we are reading about.

Today, we begin with a form of *Lectio Divina.*

The Exercise:

     1. Release your worries and concerns for this time.

     2. Take three deep breaths. With your exhalations,

breathe out the things you think you know and the expectations you have on this time. With your inhalations, breathe in the Holy Spirit. Believe that you can hear from God.

3. *Read the passage below. On this first read, just try to develop a general understanding of what is going on.*

Then Jesus was led up by the Spirit into the wilderness to be tempted by the devil. **2** When he had fasted forty days and forty nights, he was hungry afterward. **3** The tempter came and said to him, "If you are the Son of God, command that these stones become bread."

4 But he answered, "It is written, 'Man shall not live by bread alone, but by every word that proceeds out of God's mouth.'"Deuteronomy 8:3

5 Then the devil took him into the holy city. He set him on the pinnacle of the temple, **6** and said to him, "If you are the Son of God, throw yourself down, for it is written,

'He will command his angels concerning you,' and,

'On their hands they will bear you up,

so that you don't dash your foot against a stone.'"

7 Jesus said to him, "Again, it is written, 'You shall not test the Lord, your God.'"

8 Again, the devil took him to an exceedingly high mountain, and showed him all the kingdoms of the world and their glory. **9** He said to him, "I will give you all of these things, if you will fall down and worship me."

10 Then Jesus said to him, "Get behind me,[a] Satan! For it is written, 'You shall worship the Lord your God, and you shall serve him only.'

11 Then the devil left him, and behold, angels came and served him.

4. *Take three more deep breaths.*

5. *Now, read the passage above again. This time be awake and aware for details, portions, and elements that jump out at you. Some think of this as a nudge from God. Others look for words and phrases that shine or sparkle. The important thing is simply being tuned in to the things that come up for you.*

6. *Take three more deep breaths.*

7. *Read it through at least one more time, continuing to be open to whatever elements seem to stand out.*

8. *Take three more deep breaths.*

9. *Now, sit with the things that came up for you. Do not rush through the process of recalling the things you noticed today.*

10. *Take three more deep breaths.*

11. *When you are ready, begin to explore why these things might have come to your attention. Is there a common thread? Something that God might be speaking to you, now, through these words?*

12. *Take three more deep breaths. Release this practice. Sit in a time of wordless union.*

13. *If you wish, spend some time in prayer, thanking God for opening your eyes.*

DAY 2: A BREATH PRAYER

Background: A breath prayer begins with a single statement or group of statements. These words are repeated through the time dedicated to the contemplative practice. Often, one part of the statement is paired with the inhale. The other part of the statement is paired with the exhale.

Today's breath prayer comes from the passage we read yesterday. We will follow Jesus words and first say with the inhale "I do not live by bread alone" Then, with the exhale, we will add, "I will live by every word that comes out of God's mouth."

That first phrase is a good way to begin to think about fasting. Recall that there is an appendix specifically focused on the subject of fasting. This statement has lots of important implications, though, regardless on how you feel about fasting and regardless of whether you will fast or not this season.

It is easy, I think, to receive that second phrase in a way that lends itself to a narrow understanding. Sometimes, the first interpretation we take about the phrase, 'The word of God' is to think of the bible. Interpreted in this way, it is tempting to hear that second phrase as an admonition to simply read the bible and take the bible in as literal a manner as possible.

When I do this breath prayer, that is not how I understand this phrase. I begin with the idea that Jesus is said to be the word of God. Thus, when I commit myself to proceeding, or living by every word that comes out of God's mouth, I am committing myself to following Jesus. Additionally, I believe that God still speaks. On very rare occasions his words come to me quite directly during times of meditation and prayer. More often, his words come to me through nature and the love, actions, and counsel of the people around me. These are also words of God I commit myself to follow.

The Exercise:

1. *Place your feet flat on the floor.*
2. *Place your hand on your abdomen. Feel your belly move away from the spine as you inhale, filling the bottoms of the lungs first.*
3. *Feel your belly move toward the spine as you thoroughly exhale.*
4. *With the next inhale, think, "I do not live by bread alone."*
5. *Exhale.*
6. *Repeat steps 4 and 5 through several breaths.*
7. *With the next inhale, release those words.*
8. *With the next exhale, think, "I will live by every word that comes out of God's mouth." If you can, hold a wide view of the sorts of things that count as words from God.*
9. *Repeat steps 7 and 8 through several breaths.*
10. *When you are ready, bring the two phrases together.*
11. *With the inhale, think, "I do not live by bread alone."*
12. *With the exhale, think, I will live by every word that comes out of God's mouth."*
13. *Devote most of the time remaining to steps 11 and 12.*
14. *When you are ready, release these words.*

DAY 3: VISUALIZATION

Background: Visualizations are journeys that begin with the words written by someone else. Often, these words are not much more than a setting. The most successful experiences I have had with visualizations are the times I accessed some child-like imagination and playfulness and allowed myself to go beyond where those written words would have taken me if I had just stuck with the script. Like most spiritual practices, it is wise to begin a visualization by reading through the entire description to get a big picture about what, specifically, is going to happen. After that first read through, I will then engage the practice.

After reading through the whole thing, I recommend re-reading a few sentences, then picturing what they describe. Taking the suggestions about sensory input is a very important part of the process. Do not rush through experiencing the temperatures, textures, tastes, and sounds of these words. If your imagination takes you some where new, continue to ask yourself what it feels, smells, and sounds like where you are.

The visualizations in this book will be written in a narrative format. Unlike the other practices, they will not be broken down into steps.

Today's visualization is rooted in the fact that Jesus' baptism occurred just before his time in the desert. Great journeys are often begun in a ritual such as this one. I hope that today's visualization commemorates the beginning of your Lenten journey.

The Exercise:

Find yourself sitting at a table on the shore of a beautiful lake. It is almost uncomfortably warm. But a gentle breeze comes in carry-

ing dampness and cooling it to a nearly perfect temperature. The sky is so very blue. If you would like, loved ones are nearby. They do not have to be.

You get up and look to the stone staircase. This lead down and into the lake. Over and around these steps is an elaborate gate, a sort of trellis. Vines and flowers are woven into it. The grass is soft under your bare feet. You walk to the gate and open it.

The first several steps are above the water line. The stones are smooth, but much firmer than the grass. At the third step you find yourself ankle deep. The water is only a bit of a shock.

On the fourth step you look up to meet the gaze of a kind teacher. It might be someone you know. It could be Jesus. The person might not be alive now. And yet, they are here with you. The teacher smiles. You smile. You are knee deep, now, in the refreshing water.

When you are chest deep, you are next to the teacher. The teacher's arms are firm. You trust them as you lean back and are, lowered all the way into the water. There is some fear. It is unnatural to be underwater, trusting in another. The teacher, of course, lifts you back up.

"This is my wonderful child. I am well pleased in them." *Where are those words coming from? You cannot be sure.*

This strange lake does not get deeper than this. You are not meant to go back out the gate you came in, today. Walk across the lake. The teacher will come with you while you are in the water. He might speak to you. You might hear the words the teacher says.

This is the beginning of an adventure. You will return to this shore you set out from. But not today. Eventually you reach that far end of the lake. What waits for you there? Will the teacher come with you? Continue this visualization if you wish.

DAY 4: EMPTYING THE MIND

There is mystery in the heart of Easter. To us, Jesus was dead for three days. We can propose our theories of what happened during those three days. We can theorize around what it all means, and how it works.

But they are mysteries. Day 4 of each grouping will be a time to sit in silence before Mystery.

As stated in the introduction, this is a book which is both Christ-centered and interspiritual. Many of the practices on day 4 of each grouping in particular will be borrowed from our Buddhist sisters and brothers.

Once, finding information was hard. Those of us who remember life before the internet know that once we had to research with card catalogs and microfiche readers. At that time, the challenge was to locate anything at all on certain topics.

Today, our problem is quite the opposite. The internet overloads us. It is hard to imagine a topic which would not turn over results. The issue, of course, is knowing which information is relevant and reliable. It is no longer about finding information. It is about filtering the excess so that we can get to what is useful.

Our brains are a lot like an internet search. They can provide an overabundance of information. Some of it is critical. Other information? Useless and unreliable. While our brain shares with us intuitions about this person we just met or pleasing sensory data which might help us to enjoy the moment it is also reporting our fears about tomorrow, and regrets about yesterday. It might be replaying a script that no long applies.

This is one of the reasons that contemplation is so important. Many spiritual practices seek to turn down the volume of the brains constant broadcasts so that we can discern where the important information is. Today's spiritual practice calls on us to label the thinking that is going on.

It is important to remember that our brain's job is to think. It is unlikely we will achieve a goal of thoughtlessness. This would be a dubious goal anyway. My goal is to turn down the volume, not to turn it off.

The Exercise:

1. *Release your expectations and sense of obligations with your exhale.*
2. *Inhale through the nose.*
3. *Exhale through the mouth.*
4. *Seek a time of mental quiet.*
5. *When a thought arises, gently label it "thinking."*
6. *return to your breath.*
7. *Continue this breathing, labeling of thoughts, and returning to the mental quiet for the time you have set aside for your practice this morning.*

DAY 5: APOPHATIC MEDITATION

Background: Apophatic meditations are designed to help us deal with the paradoxical nature of reality. These are built around 3-sentence cycles: an affirmation, a negation, and a negation of the negation.

For example, a cycle might be, "God is love." (affirmation)

"God is not love" (negation)

And "God is not-not love." (negation of the negation)

Apophatic meditations are not easy. The third sentence—the negation of the negation—can be the most difficult. There is more to be said about this practice in general and the third sentence in particular. But sometimes, it is best to jump in and begin a thing without getting too bogged down in attempts at explanation. Today, we will do just this: jump and do it. We will return to the meaning of the negation of the negation for day 10.

The cycles chosen this week are general ones which explore the relationship of Jesus with ourselves and the other aspects of *God.*

The Exercise:

1. *Take three deep breaths.*

2. *With your next inhale, think, "I am in Christ."*

3. *With your next exhale, think, "I am not in Christ."*

4. *With your next inhale, think "I am not not in Christ."*

5. *Exhale.*

6. *With your next inhale, think, "Christ is in me."*

7. *With your next exhale, think, "Christ is not in me."*

8. *With your next inhale, think, "Christ is not not in me."*

9. *Exhale.*

10. *With your next inhale, think "Jesus is Christ."*

11. *With your next exhale, think, "Jesus is not Christ."*

12. *With your next inhale, think, "Jesus is not not Christ."*

13. *Exhale.*

14. *With your next inhale, think "Jesus is God."*

15. *With your next exhale, think "Jesus is not God."*

16. *With your next inhale, think, "Jesus is not not God."*

17. *Exhale.*

18. *Repeat steps 1-17, as you have time.*

SECOND GROUPING

Traditionally, Lent has focused on two different events. The first is Jesus' 40 days in the desert. The second is a focus on the crucifixion, death, and resurrection. On the surface, this might seem like an odd pair of events to pair together. They did not occur particularly close together. They don't have lots of obvious components in common.

There is a deep wisdom in placing them together, though. The time in the desert seems to foreshadow Jesus' death on the cross. Many understandings of the crucifixion understand this act to have been connected in some way to Satan and evil. Though the personification of evil does not appear anywhere else in the Gospels, many see him as an important behind the scenes figure at the end of the story.

Myths, epics, and heroic tales often feature a scene near the beginning which introduces the protagonist and foreshadows the battle to come. Contemporary epics continue this tradition. I still get chills when watching the Empire Strikes Back. Han and friends wander into a room expecting a nice dinner. They are suddenly face-to-face with Darth Vader. Near the beginning of the last of the Harry Potter books and films, Harry and friends are flying away from the house they had been staying at. We expect an action scene with a few of the master villain's henchmen.

There are some who would say that the Gospels follow in this tradition. There are others who would suggest that all our ancient and modern epics are in some ways echoes of this primal story. I don't want to get involved in that particular question here. The important thing is that either way, this element of mythology is at work in the Jesus story.

A difference ought to be noted in how this plays out, though. Most of the time, in both modern and ancient stories, there is some measure of defeat in this early battle. In the Star Wars movie, Han Solo and company are captured. In Harry Potter, Hedwig, his longtime owl-companion, is killed.

Jesus wins a personal victory in the desert. Though he is in need of the angel's care, he faces off with the enemy and wins. The victory that occurs at the end of the story seems to be of a different magnitude. After Jesus' return, it suddenly seems to apply to us in some way.

This week, we will continue to focus on Jesus' battle in the desert. But it is worth keeping in mind that despite the appearance to the contrary, these two Lenten foci are not isolated events. There is a real connection here.

DAY 6: SACRED READING PRACTICE

Background: We continue with the passage we began with. This week we will try a holy imagining practice with it. As you will see, there are differences between this practice and *Lectio Divina*.

One of the important things to note about holy imagining is that this is not a fact-finding activity. A degree in biblical archaeology is not required. Picturing the scene vividly is a powerful experience. But the idea is not to discover what happened. The idea is to live in the words of the text and do our best to experience the passage in a new, visceral way.

The Exercise:

1. Release your expectations and stress with your first exhalations. Breathe in a sense of God's Holy Spirit with your inhalations. Continue this for as many breaths as feels right.

2. Read the passage below. The first time through, seek only to remind yourself of the overarching narrative scope of the passage.

Then Jesus was led up by the Spirit into the wilderness to be tempted by the devil. **2** When he had fasted forty days and forty nights, he was hungry afterward. **3** The tempter came and said to him, "If you are the Son of God, command that these stones become bread."

4 But he answered, "It is written, 'Man shall not live by bread alone, but by every word that proceeds out of God's mouth.'"Deuteronomy 8:3

5 Then the devil took him into the holy city. He set him on the pinnacle of the temple, **6** and said to him, "If you are the Son of God, throw yourself down, for it is written,

'He will command his angels concerning you,' and,

'On their hands they will bear you up,

so that you don't dash your foot against a stone.'"

7 Jesus said to him, "Again, it is written, 'You shall not test the Lord, your God.'"

8 Again, the devil took him to an exceedingly high mountain, and showed him all the kingdoms of the world and their glory. **9** He said to him, "I will give you all of these things, if you will fall down and worship me."

10 Then Jesus said to him, "Get behind me,[a] Satan! For it is written, 'You shall worship the Lord your God, and you shall serve him only.'

11 Then the devil left him, and behold, angels came and served him.

3. Now, read it as it appears below. Interspersed in the text are several prompts in italics. These are opportunities to furnish sensory information into our imagining of the passage. There may be several places you can find places to furnish additional details. As you read through, take your time with this. Let the scene expand and play itself out in your mind.

Then Jesus was led up by the Spirit into the wilderness to be tempted by the devil.

What did this leading look like? Could Jesus see the Spirit? Could others? See Jesus walking into the wilderness. Note the set of his shoulders. Hear his sandals on the ground.

2 When he had fasted forty days and forty nights, he was hungry afterward.

See Jesus' haggard expression. Feel the rumbling deep within of being so very famished. Look through Jesus' eyes. See the Tempter come upon you in this state. What are the feelings and expressions that pass between them?

3 The tempter came and said to him, "If you are the Son of God, command that these stones become bread."

4 But he answered, "It is written, 'Man shall not live by bread alone, but by every word that proceeds out of God's mouth.'

Hear these words. Give a tone and expression to them. Is the Tempter smooth or forceful? Is Jesus invigorated by this or exhausted? Is he matter of fact of triumphant?

5 Then the devil took him into the holy city. He set him on the pinnacle of the temple, **6** and said to him, "If you are the Son of God, throw yourself down, for it is written,

'He will command his angels concerning you,' and,

'On their hands they will bear you up,

so that you don't dash your foot against a stone.'"

7 Jesus said to him, "Again, it is written, 'You shall not test the Lord, your God.'"

Do they teleport? How do they get there? Look, slowly at the beautiful temple beneath your feet. Now, turn your gaze to this magnificent city. See the birds flying over the rooftops. The clouds in the sky.

Does Jesus pick up steam, here? Is there a sense of increased assurance? Or has Jesus been assured all the way through.

8 Again, the devil took him to an exceedingly high mountain, and showed him all the kingdoms of the world and their glory. **9** He said to him, "I will give you all of these things, if you will fall down and worship me."

Feel the wind ruffle your clothes. Smell the vegetation's scents being blown to you. Behold all the kingdoms you are overlooking. Experience the things Jesus might have.

10 Then Jesus said to him, "Get behind me,[a] Satan! For it is written, 'You shall worship the Lord your God, and you shall serve him only.'

11 Then the devil left him, and behold, angels came and served him.

4.   Read through the original passage (presented below for your convenience) again at a leisurely pace. Furnish the details you just did. See if there is anything else to add.

Then Jesus was led up by the Spirit into the wilderness to be tempted by the devil. **2** When he had fasted forty days and forty nights, he was hungry afterward. **3** The tempter came and said to him, "If you are the Son of God, command that these stones become bread."

4 But he answered, "It is written, 'Man shall not live by bread alone, but by every word that proceeds out of God's mouth.' Deuteronomy

5 Then the devil took him into the holy city. He set him on the pinnacle of the temple, **6** and said to him, "If you are the Son of God, throw yourself down, for it is written,

   'He will command his angels concerning you,' and,

   'On their hands they will bear you up,

      so that you don't dash your foot against a stone.'"

7 Jesus said to him, "Again, it is written, 'You shall not test the Lord, your God.'"

8 Again, the devil took him to an exceedingly high mountain, and showed him all the kingdoms of the world and their glory. **9** He said to him, "I will give you all of these things, if you will fall down and worship me."

10 Then Jesus said to him, "Get behind me,[a] Satan! For it is written, 'You shall worship the Lord your God, and you shall serve him only.'

11 Then the devil left him, and behold, angels came and served him.

5. *Inhale. Exhale. Repeat this three times.*

6.   *Consider what new thoughts or experiences you have about this passage after having lived through it with your senses.*

DAY 7: A BREATH PRAYER

Background: There is a long list of things we might wish to be free from. Some possible things we might wish to be free from include temptation, stress, fear, depression, disappointment, vice, anger, worry, evil, sin, Satan, darkness, confusion, insecurity. There is a parallel list of things we might wish to be filled with. A partial list here might include strength, relaxation, bravery, hope, acceptance, virtue, love, contentment, goodness, Jesus, light, understanding, and self-confidence.

We are still in the early stages on our Lenten journey. Today, I would like to encourage you to think about what your hopes are for these 40 days. What do you wish to be ride of? What do you wish you could have more of? Breath prayers can be used to visualize this process. They can be especially powerful when connected with the body.

I have chosen to write the description below for someone who wishes to be free of stress and filled with love. Recognize that you can choose anything off the lists above, or anything that I might have missed. The exercise might feel more natural if the two elements seem like opposites. For example, filling our life with light and ridding ourselves of darkness might feel more natural than filling ourselves with light and ridding ourselves of temptation.

The Exercise.

1. *Begin with three deep breaths.*

2. *With your next exhale, see the stress from your feet and ankles being blown out of your body with the air.*

3. *With your next inhale, fill that now-empty space in your feet and ankles with love.*

4. *With your next exhale, blow out the stress from your shins and calves.*

5. *With the next inhale, fill the calves, shins, and feet with love.*

6. *Exhale the stress from your knees and thighs, being aware of the back of these, too.*

7. *Inhale love that fills your legs from knees to toes.*

8. *Exhale stress from the pelvis and buttocks.*

9. *Inhale love to fill the space you have made, from the waist down.*

10. *Exhale stress from the stomach and low back.*

11. *Inhale love to fill the lower half of your body.*

12. *Exhale stress from the fingers and hands.*

13. *Inhale love to fill this area.*

14. *Exhale stress from the forearm and elbows.*

15. *Inhale love to these the lower arms.*

16. *Exhale stress from the shoulders and upper arms.*

17. *Inhale love to fill the entirety of your arms.*

18. *Return your attention to the trunk. Exhale another breath of stress from the lower body.*

19. *Inhale love to fill the lower body.*

20. *Exhale stress from the chest and upper back.*

21. *Inhale love to fill the body completely below the neck.*

22. *Exhale stress from the neck and upper shoulders.*

23. *Inhale love to fill this space.*

24. *Exhale stress from the jaw, and lower parts of the face and head.*

25. *Inhale love.*

26. *Exhale stress from the upper face and head.*

27. *Take three deep breaths, exhaling residual stress, inhaling love into those places where space was made.*

DAY 8: A VISUALIZATION

Background: Visualizations can seem deceptively simple. There are not instructions on these practices, unlike the other practices in this book. For many of the visualizations in this book, there will be a pair of challenges that does not occur with the other practices. These two challenges in some sense offset the apparent simplicity.

The first challenge is to fully enter the scene. Because there are no step-by-step instructions, it can be tempting to gloss over this practice. If we read these at a surface level, they will impact us at a surface level. That is not a bad thing. But I suspect it is not the reason you are reading this book. Reading a passage with urgency balanced with slowness, allowing our imagination to expand upon the scene, drinking in the fullness of the sensory details... all these are ways to allow ourselves to be vulnerable and changed by these visualizations. Approaching these visualizations with a humility and an awareness that God is active here will be beneficial visualization while simultaneously applying it to ourselves. Many visualizations are metaphors of a sort. Some of the power they wield is in how we apply it to ourselves.

Interpreting a metaphor begins with the literal. If we did not know what that a rose is beautiful and that it has thorns, we would not be able to do much with the statement, "My love is a red rose." On the other hand, if we got stuck on only the rose, and did not reflect about our love, we would also be missing out.

Today, we will visualize Jesus' fast, and his being tended to by the angels. This is a powerful thing to do. But it will be even more powerful if you can begin with this image and then apply it to yourself. In what ways have you been on a 40 day fast? What would it look like if the angels were tending you?

Jesus spent 40 days in the desert fasting. Begin by going back forty days in your own mind. Think back to forty days before today. Spend just a minute thinking about the length of time forty days is. Consider the things you have accomplished. Feel the length of this duration.

Now, imagine Jesus going for this length of time. Not eating. Not drinking. Not connecting with any other people. See him hungry, tired, bored and lonely. But also, perhaps close to God. Triumphant. Focusing on himself and his connection to his father.

Bring the senses into this time. See the skin tighten across his jaw. Hear his feet on the desert sand. Feel the scratchy rocks emanating a heat after the sun has set. See the giant moon hanging in the sky. If it was full when Jesus went into the desert, Jesus would have watched it wax and wane through each of its phases over those 40 days.

Let Jesus in your mind's eye do whatever he might have done. Do not rush this part. Perhaps it will take most of the time you have set aside for your spiritual practice today. We know the end of the story. It must not have been all fun and games. He needed the angel's love and care at the end of his time.

See those angels come. Are they beautiful men with bird wings, like a medieval painting? Creatures covered in too many eyes, so monstrous they always begin with "Do not fear?" See them care for Jesus and nurse him back to health.

As you wrap up this time place yourself in Jesus position. Leaving behind responsibilities and day-to-day expectations in a manner that might be liberating. But abstaining from things we need for forty long days. Would you go to a desert for 40 days? Could you? Is it possible that in some ways you already are?

Let yourself, in your mind's eye, do whatever is that you would do for forty days. Do not rush through this stage either. If I was there, I would be tired and weak at the end. I suspect this is true of you, too. Let yourself fall into the loving embrace of the angels, now. They will bring you back to health.

DAY 9: CLEARING THE MIND

Background: Father Thomas Keating has popularized a practice that is rooted in a centuries-old book called 'The Cloud of Unknowing.'

It begins with the choice of a sacred word. It should be noted that this sacred word might be an image, or even the breath itself. The instructions below presume the practitioner is going the word-route. Some of the more popular words chosen include "Love" "Loved" "Spirit" "God" and "Yahweh." Before you begin, it is wise to have chosen your sacred word. You should stick with your sacred word at least through the duration of your practice.

Proponents of centering prayer advocate working up to 2-30-minute sessions each day.

Exercise

1. *Place your feet flat on the floor and relax.*
2. *Say your sacred word. Recognize that this is your consent to the holy spirit to come and meet with you.*
3. *As best you can, clear your mind.*
4. *Know that thoughts and feelings are bound to arise. Each time they do, dismiss them gently by saying your sacred word.*
5. *Set a goal of continuing this practice for at least 20 minutes; half an hour is even better.*

DAY 10: APOPHATIC MEDITATION

Background Information: Recall that apophatic meditation is comprised of 3 phrase cycles. Each begins with an affirmation, such as 'God is love.' It moves on to a negation, such as 'God is not love'. It concludes with the negation of the negation: 'God is not not love.'

It is clear what the first two phrases mean. There is some limited value in exploring some things that the third statement means. This value is limited because we are operating in the realm of the word-transcendent, here. That is part of the meaning of the term 'apophatic' itself. The apophatic is that which is beyond meaning and words.

One way of getting at the value of that third sentence is to consider what apophatic meditation would be like without it. If I simply first thought, "God is love." And then followed it up with "God is not love." It would seem like I had simply changed my mind. It would appear that I had corrected my original judgement. By adding the third statement I am claiming that both of the first claims are true, and, neither of them is true.

Holding a paradox without resolving it is a very difficult thing to do. In many aspects of our lives it is not helpful. When we are driving, we need to decide if we are going to turn left or go straight. When we are working, we need to decide if we will go after the big promotion or be satisfied with where we are. There are times that we must choose this or that. For the most part, we are quite good at this.

But most of us are not very good at recognizing that the world is paradoxical. There are advantages to both sides of an argument, often. There is truth and falsehood in the stories we tell ourselves. There are lots of activities that help us get better at choosing this or that. I do not know of many which help us get better at affirming the both/and.

Meditation in general is one of those rare activities that builds this ability quite effectively. In my opinion, no method of contemplation does this better than apophatic meditation. This growth in nondualistic thinking comes from the third sentence, the negation of the negation. That third sentence means lots of different things. Some little sense of these comes with differences in punctuation and formatting. As a result, when I am sharing apophatic meditations, I do not adopt a single, standard convention. It is difficult to use words to spell these precise differences out. But spend a minute with each of these negations of the negation. See if you can feel some of the subtle differences between them:

God is not not love.

God is not-not love.

God is not not-love.

God is *not* not love.

God is *not* not-love.

The Exercise

1. *Release your concerns and expectations for this time,*
2. *Inhale. Exhale.*
3. *With your next inhale, think, "God is father."*

4. *With your next exhale, think, "God is not father."*
5. *With your next inhale, think "God is not not father."*
6. *Exhale.*
7. *Inhale. Exhale.*
8. *With your next inhale, think "Jesus is son."*
9. *With your next exhale, think "Jesus is not son."*
10. *With your next inhale, think "Jesus is not-not son."*
11. *Exhale.*
12. *Inhale. Exhale.*
13. *With your next inhale, think "The holy spirit is the third person."*
14. *With your next exhale think, "The holy spirit is not the third person."*
15. *With your next inhale think, "The holy Spirit is not not-the third person."*
16. *Exhale.*
17. *Inhale. Exhale.*
18. *With your next inhale, think "God is one."*
19. *With your next exhale think "God is not one."*
20. *With your next inhale think, "God is not not one."*
21. *Exhale.*
22. *Inhale. Exhale.*
23. *With your next inhale think, "God is three."*
24. *With your next exhale think "God is not three."*
25. *With your next inhale think "God is not not three."*
26. *Exhale.*
27. *Inhale. Exhale.*
28. *With your next inhale think, "God is three in one."*
29. *With your next exhale think "God is not three in one."*
30. *With your next inhale think "God is not not three in one."*

THIRD GROUPING

For me, Lent is a time that begins in light and knowing. This is the cataphatic. It slowly becomes about darkness and mystery. It moves into the apophatic.

To the extent that it is about Jesus' forty days in the desert, we are not told much about the fast itself. We can only imagine that at some point, it begins to grow difficult.

As for the other narrative Lent is focused on in the beginning, Jesus leads his followers triumphantly into Jerusalem. There is drama, pageantry, and theatre here. The crowds are declaring the great things that are about to be done. Jesus takes some of their expectations about a hero returning from war and turns them all on their heads. It begins with the appearance that Jesus is in charge.

And slowly, it slides into the unknown, The darkness, the lack of control. It seems to be a thing that goes beyond words, meaning, and understanding. At some point, this cataphatic tale becomes apophatic.

In the introduction, I noted that working toward thirty minutes of meditation a day is a worthy goal. It might be that you began with sits of just a few minutes. Nearly every practice is do-able for just a few minutes. If you have been punishing yourself to extend your endurance and time of sitting, it might be that you are reaching a point with some practices that it is difficult to do the same one for the entire time you had planned on dedicating to contemplation.

As the time of your session moves toward half an hour, it is worth considering whether you ought to split the time between two sessions. Generally speaking, I would not recommend splitting a session between more than two practices. And it is worth being on the alert for the phenomenon related to one we discussed earlier. Recall that in the introduction we began with the realization that committing to a practice for a certain length of time is a valuable thing to do. This prevents us from stopping a practice just when things are getting uncomfortable. When it is possible, working through the discomfort is where growth happens.

Just as we can try and run away from growth by ending our session, we can also run away from growth by switching practices too often or too soon. If I begin a new practice today and simply have the plan that I will do this until I am bored, and then I switch to some other practice, I am still running away from growth. When I switch over to the second practice, I have allowed myself to retreat from the things I would do better to face.

Having said all this, I wish to repeat something that came up earlier in this volume: be kind to yourself. If you are distressed, do not subject yourself to more pain than is necessary.

DAY 11: SACRED READING

Background: Our Holy Reading practices are drawn from two traditions: Lectio Divina and Holy Imaging. Today, we explore a different approach to lectio. The result of this particular practice is the discovery of a breath prayer in the words we are reading.

Like many forms of Lectio, this asks us to be on the alert for that still, small voice of God. It asks us to be alert to the reactions that stir within. In the case of today's practice, we are on the lookout for some words that bare repeating, some things that we would benefit by hearing.

This is a deeply transferable skill. One of the benefits of this practice is that when we learn to trust our ability to hear God when we read a certain passage, we build the ability to trust ourselves in other aspects of life.

There can be a temptation to look for the things that instantly make us feel good. This isn't a bad thing. There is nothing wrong with feeling good. But feeling that stirring within is not the same as feeling good. It might be that the section troubles or confuses us. Some of my most powerful experiences with Lectio have been when I sat with the parts of the text I was not so comfortable with, when I wrestled with words or phrases that did not neatly fit my narrative.

In some cases, when I have focused on these difficult portions, I have come to a new understanding of what the words might mean. In other cases, I have been challenged to adjust my preconditioned assumptions.

The Practice
1. *Place your feet flat on the floor. Take three deep breaths.*
2. *Read through the passage below. On this first reading, just read it to get a sense of the overall story.*

When they came near to Jerusalem and came to Bethsphage,[a] to the Mount of Olives, then Jesus sent two disciples, 2 saying to them, "Go into the village that is opposite you, and immediately you will find a donkey tied, and a colt with her. Untie them and bring them to me. 3 If anyone says anything to you, you shall say, 'The Lord needs them,' and immediately he will send them."

4 All this was done that it might be fulfilled which was spoken through the prophet, saying,

5

"Tell the daughter of Zion,
    behold, your King comes to you,
    humble, and riding on a donkey,
on a colt, the foal of a donkey." Zechariah 9:9
6 The disciples went and did just as Jesus commanded them, 7 and brought the donkey and the colt and laid their clothes on them; and he sat on them. 8 A very great multitude spread their clothes on the road. Others cut branches from the trees and spread them on the road. 9 The multitudes who went in front of him, and those who followed, kept shouting, "Hosanna[b] to the son of David! Blessed is he who comes in the name of the Lord! Hosanna in the highest!" Psalm 118:26
10 When he had come into Jerusalem, all the city was stirred up, saying, "Who is this?"

11 The multitudes said, "This is the prophet, Jesus, from Nazareth of Galilee."

12 Jesus entered into the temple of God and drove out all of those who sold and bought in the temple, and overthrew the money changers' tables and the seats of those who sold the doves. 13 He said to them, "It is written, 'My house shall be called a house of prayer,' Isaiah 56:7 but you have made it a den of robbers!" Jere-

miah 7:11

14 The lame and the blind came to him in the temple, and he healed them. **15** But when the chief priests and the scribes saw the wonderful things that he did, and the children who were crying in the temple and saying, "Hosanna to the son of David!" they were indignant, **16** and said to him, "Do you hear what these are saying?"

Jesus said to them, "Yes. Did you never read, 'Out of the mouth of children and nursing babies, you have perfected praise?'"Psalm 8:2

17 He left them and went out of the city to Bethany, and camped there.

3. *Reread the passage. This time be on the lookout. You are looking for a grouping of about 1-10 words that speak to you. If you get to the end of the passage and did not find anything, read the passage a third time, slower. Perhaps you will read through it a fourth, too.*

4. *Choose 1-10 words. Say these words with the breath. You might assign all of the words to the inhale. You might split them between the inhale and the exhale. You might assign them all to the exhalation.*

5. *Devote a significant portion of the time you have left to this practice, of focusing on this word.*

6. *When you are ready, release these words. Sit in a time of wordless union.*

DAY 12: A BREATH PRAYER

If you did yesterday's practice, you constructed a breath prayer of your own from the verses we are focused on. It might be that you wish to return to that breath prayer today. If the time you spent with those verses yesterday was helpful, I would like to encourage you to do just that. Go back to yesterday's practice.

If you would rather try something new and different, I would like to invite you to try the breath prayer that was waiting for me, when I engaged that text with a Lectio Divina practice.

The Exercise
1. *Relax. Take 3 deep breaths.*
2. *With your next inhale, think, "Who is this?"*
3. *With your next exhale, think, "This is Jesus."*
4. *Repeat steps 3 and 4 for most of the time you have set aside for this practice today.*
5. *When you are ready, release these words. Sit in a time or wordless union.*

DAY 13:
VISUALIZATION

Background: Often, when we visualize an event, there is a desire to place it in an either/or category.

Harry Potter captures this well. Near the climax of the entire series, events occur in another world, away from the action. The things that occur there do not seem possible. The title character asks, "Was this real? Or is it happening in my head?"

The sage-like Albus Dumbledore answers "Of course it is happening inside your head, Harry, but why on earth should that mean that it is not real?"

This is a helpful way to enter visualizations. Perhaps they are the place where our minds intersect with something bigger than us. But even if it is only us... This too, is real.

The more the senses are engaged in visualizations, the more powerful they tend to be. When they leave the setting open to your own history, it can be wonderful to return to a setting that you have fond memories of, perhaps a place that you cannot easily go back to.

In today's exercise, you will be invited to meet with Jesus. Perhaps you will substitute this appearance with someone else. Maybe you don't have a name for Spirit as Spirit shows up.

Lots can be reaped out of this experience if we resist the temptation to turn this into a historical quest. Getting caught up on the details we don't know can sour this experience.

Spiritual Exercise

1. *Place your feet flat on the floor. Breathe.*
2. *Choose a setting you know well. Preferably an outside environment.*
3. *After you have recalled what this place looks like, furnish the sounds. Feel the temperature of the air. Consider the smells.*
4. *See yourself walking along a path in this special place.*
5. *Feel yourself approached by a figure. This is Jesus. Jesus will be walking with you, today.*
6. *It might be a while before Jesus speaks. Perhaps there won't be any words at all.*
7. *Continue the walk for as long as you would like. Enjoy your time with him.*

DAY 14: EMPTYING THE MIND

Background: Any word, repeated enough, begins to sound like nonsense.

It seems to me that when we use a word only once or twice, we have an easy time mistaking the letter-sounds for the thing those letters stand for. But as we repeat the word, we come face-to-face with the fact that the sounds are arbitrary. For example, when we say the word 'cat' once, we get a picture in our mind. But when we say the word repeatedly, we are reminded there is nothing inherent to those letters that connects them to the animal. It is merely an agreement that more-or-less randomly assigned these particularly sounds.

Saying a word over and over, creates a sort-of white noise, for me. It begins with the meaning of the word. But slowly even this fades into the background, leaving me in a state beyond words.

Exercise

1. *Place your feet flat on the floor.*
2. *Choose your sacred word.*
3. *Say the word. Out loud, if possible. Say it without ceasing. Say it a calm, measured rate; say it as many times as you can with each exhale. Think it or mouth it as many times as you can with each inhale.*
4. *If you find yourself distracted by thoughts or feelings, return your attention to the saying of that single word.*

DAY 15: APOPHATIC MEDITATION

There is a strange relationship between apophatic meditation and breath prayers. Breath prayers tend to be light, airy, and word dependent. On the other hand, as the name apophatic indicates these forms of meditation tend to be word transcendent. At the most concrete level, in a breath prayer we are only focused on the affirmation. It is only in the apophatic meditation that we subject the statement to negation and negation of the negation.

Nonetheless, both use a limited number of phrases and they are often repeated. Each leads to releasing the concerns and clearing the minds. Today, we will employ some phrases in an apophatic meditation that we will later apply to a breath prayer. It is worth noticing the ways that the effects of these methods are similar, and the ways that the effects of these methods are quite different.

As you move forward into your spiritual practice, this might be a place to explore further. When you discover a great breath prayer, try it as an apophatic meditation. Or, of course, when you discover a great apophatic meditation, try it out as a breath prayer.

A few words are in order about the details of this practice as written today. First off, one of the struggles with apophatic meditation is that sometimes it is difficult to know to do with the breath. Many ways of configuring apophatic meditation result in most of the sentences being coordinated with the inhale. If, for example, we begin with the affirmation on an inhale, then the negation lands on the exhale, but then the negation of the negation lands on the inhale again. In a scenario like this one, two-thirds of the "action" is coordinated to the inhalations.

Sometimes when I finish a group of cycles of apophatic meditations, I find myself wishing for a little more symmetry. One solution to this problem is to hold the breath. This means that both the inhalation and the exhalation end up with a single phrase each. It also underscores the urgency and the strangeness of the negation of the negation, as it is accompanied with a rather unnatural task.

A second consideration regarding this apophatic meditation: Some of these sentences seem a little strange. For example, the first sentence below is "Jesus was born." While this affirmation is probably not particularly troublesome, but what comes next is, "Jesus was not born."

Trying on statements like this is one of the gifts of apophatic meditation. I don't know about you, but my initial response to the statement, "Jesus was not born." Is to think, "Well, that's kind of stupid. Of course, Jesus was born."

But when I sit with this statement, the first thing that comes up for me is that I realize that there is a Jesus in my mind. On a good day, this Jesus bares a bit of resemblance to the Jesus who once lived. But truthfully, the Jesus who lives in my mind was not physically born in this world. Sitting with the sentence awakens me to that reality.

In other words, sometimes sitting with the negation to an apparently self-evident statement helps us to realize the limits and problems we never before explored. Perhaps these statements are not quite so self-evident after all.

The Exercise

1. *Release your stress and worries for the duration of this exercise.*

2. *With your next inhale, think, "Jesus was born."*

3. *With your next exhale, think "Jesus was not born."*

4. *Holding the breath, think, "Jesus was not-not born."*

5. *Inhale.*

6. *Exhale.*

7. *With your next inhale, think, "Jesus is alive."*

8. *With your exhale, think, "Jesus is not alive."*

9. *Hold your breath and think "Jesus is not-not alive."*

10. *Inhale.*

11. *Exhale.*

12. *With your next inhale, think, "Jesus is on the cross."*

13. *With your next exhale, think "Jesus is not on the cross."*

14. *Hold your breath, and think, "Jesus is not-not on the cross."*

15. *Inhale.*

16. *Exhale.*

17. *With your next inhale, think "Jesus is dead."*

18. *With your next exhale, think, "Jesus is not dead."*

19. *Hold your breath and think "Jesus is not-not dead."*

20. *Inhale.*

21. *Exhale.*

22. *With your next inhale, think "Jesus is returned."*

23. *With your next exhale, think "Jesus is not returned."*

24. *Hold the breath. Think, "Jesus is not not returned."*

25. *If you wish, repeat these apophatic meditations. When you are*

ready, release these words and sit in a time of union.

FOURTH GROUPING

We find ourselves now halfway through lent. I hope that you are finding new ways of understanding what this season is. The challenging thing for some of us is that we are raised in a world which believes that nearly everything can be expressed with words. I suspect this is why many people feel that "doing theology" -- arguing about God and studying beliefs and history about this topic-- is the best way to follow Jesus.

Even after I began meditating, I wanted to try and put these experiences into words. As I tried to tell people who were not contemplatives what my experiences were like, I noticed the expressions on their face. It was like when I try to talk about a dream that felt so strange and powerful, but it just has no context or resonance with my audience. Or describing what I did on vacation. The other person was simply not there.

Sharing with others through those words was a way that experiences began to feel real to me. I did not realize that one of the reasons that contemplative practices are necessary in the first place is precisely because there are some experiences which cannot be expressed with words. When I realized this, I discovered that engaging in these practices with someone I love is often much more rewarding than talking about these experiences with someone I love and writing about how to do these practices took the place of describing what they are like for me.

It might be that no new understandings are arising for you. This does not mean that you are doing it wrong. It is simply the way of these things. But if something new is happening in your soul, if you a new understanding is unfolding, it might be difficult or impossible to express this with words. It might be helpful to meditate with a friend and share in these gifts that way.

There have been three opportunities now, to practice each of the types of spiritual practice. Probably, there are some types of practice which feel easier. There are presumably others which are more challenging. Much more will be said about this later, but as you continue in these practices, I would like to encourage you to begin to think not only the practices that feel good and easy for you. Think also about the practices that are doing good in you. These might not be the easy ones.

DAY 16: SACRED READING PRACTICE

Today, we return to holy imaging. Perhaps the distinctions between holy imagining and lectio Divina are becoming clearer. As the name implies, holy imagining relies on the imagination to bring us a deeper appreciation of what is going on in a text. Lectio Dvina challenges us to find specific aspects of the text which speak to us.

There tends to be a more explicit reference to the actions of the Holy Spirit in Lectio Divina. But it would be a mistake to think God is absent in anything we do, let alone spiritual practices.

Today, we will focus in our holy imagining practice on experiencing the scene from the perspective of someone within the narratives. When most people are asked to take on the perspective of someone within the story, they naturally gravitate toward flawed, sympathetic, and major figures. For example, in a story where Jesus interacts with pharisees and his disciples, the natural point of contact for most people would be the disciples. The disciples are flawed, sympathetic, and are specifically mentioned.

This is not a bad thing to do. But it is not the only option. Sometimes it is not even the most rewarding thing to do. One option that people tend to resist is to experience a story as through the eyes of Jesus. Please be aware that choosing to see the story from Jesus' eyes is not an act of arrogance. To want to experience the story from this perspective does not mean we are equating ourselves with Jesus in any kind of unhealthy way.

On the other hand, experiencing a story from the perspective of those who stood in Jesus' way is a difficult but incredibly powerful experience. If we get past our gut-reaction of seeing the interloper as other, we can sometimes discover that they are quite relatable.

Finally, consider whether you would like to see this scene from the perspective of someone on the sidelines. Perhaps they are named and implied. For example, if a crowd is present you might take on the persona of some person within that crowd. On the other hand, they don't need to be specifically mentioned at all. See the scene from the eyes of an unmentioned fly, or from the stall of a vendor. Remember that this is an exercise in seeing the story in a new way, not in uncovering historical fact, and that if your imagination takes you into some experience that is outside of the scenes as described, that exciting and wonderful things can result.

The practice:
1. *Take three deep breaths.*
2. *Read through the passage below. Read it just to become aware of the scope and sequence of the events described.*

When they came near to Jerusalem and came to Bethsphage,[a] to the Mount of Olives, then Jesus sent two disciples, 2 saying to them, "Go into the village that is opposite you, and immediately you will find a donkey tied, and a colt with her. Untie them and bring them to me. 3 If anyone says anything to you, you shall say, 'The Lord needs them,' and immediately he will send them." 4 All this was done that it might be fulfilled which was spoken through the prophet, saying,

5 "Tell the daughter of Zion,

behold, your King comes to you,

humble, and riding on a donkey,
on a colt, the foal of a donkey." Zechariah 9:9
6 The disciples went and did just as Jesus commanded
them, 7 and brought the donkey and the colt and laid
their clothes on them; and he sat on them. 8 A very great
multitude spread their clothes on the road. Others cut
branches from the trees and spread them on the road.
9 The multitudes who went in front of him, and those
who followed, kept shouting, "Hosanna[b] to the son of
David! Blessed is he who comes in the name of the Lord!
Hosanna in the highest!" Psalm 118:26

\10 When he had come into Jerusalem, all the city was
stirred up, saying, "Who is this?"

11 The multitudes said, "This is the prophet, Jesus, from
Nazareth of Galilee."

12 Jesus entered into the temple of God and drove out all
of those who sold and bought in the temple, and overthrew the money changers' tables and the seats of those
who sold the doves. 13 He said to them, "It is written,
'My house shall be called a house of prayer,' Isaiah 56:7
but you have made it a den of robbers!" Jeremiah 7:11

14 The lame and the blind came to him in the temple,
and he healed them. 15 But when the chief priests and
the scribes saw the wonderful things that he did, and
the children who were crying in the temple and saying,
"Hosanna to the son of David!" they were indignant, 16
and said to him, "Do you hear what these are saying?"

Jesus said to them, "Yes. Did you never read, 'Out of the
mouth of children and nursing babies, you have perfected praise?'" Psalm 8:2

17 He left them and went out of the city to Bethany, and camped there.

3. *Now, reread the passage above. This time become aware of the perspectives it could be experienced through. It is not necessary to commit to any one just yet. Be aware of your intuitions. Remember that you could choose any figure who is either implied or explicitly mentioned.*
4. *Take three deep breaths.*
5. *Choose a perspective. If need be, read the passage again to help your decision.*
6. *Take three deep breaths.*
7. *Reread the passage a third time. Now see it through the eyes you have chosen. Try to literally see the experiences through their eyes. Imagine the sounds they would hear. The textures of their clothes on the skin.*
8. *Take three deep breaths.*
9. *Read the passage a final time... at least the portions where your figure is present. Try to keep up the awareness of their sensory experiences. What are their thoughts? Feelings? Expressions? Motivations?*
10. *Take three deep breaths.*
11. *Sit with any new experience you have of this passage. When you are ready, release these words. Spend some time with God.*

Day 17: A Breath prayer

There is a tension within Christianity in general and in Lent in particularly. That tension is rooted in the push and pull of the "already happened" and the "not yet." In its broadest strokes, this tension exists in the form of the fact that Jesus returned after his death to his followers and that he will return again.

In a sense, Jesus' return has already happened. In another sense, Jesus' return is in the category of "not yet." The existence of God's kingdom exists similarly in this category. Most of us look forward to heaven as a future reality. And yet, it is already among us.

This is less of a metaphysical leap when we recognize that we are part of a long tradition. Most of us hear the Jesus story all at once. We know that Jesus returns once, and he returns again. But to his followers, this end was not a foregone conclusion. The time between Jesus death and his resurrection were, for them, a profound experience of living in that place between the "already happened" and the "not yet."

There is a cycle built into the universe. We see it everywhere: morning, noon, night, morning again. Fall, Winter, Spring, Summer, back to the Fall. We are children, become adolescents, become adults and have children who will have their own adolescents. Success, failure, back up to success. This is the cycle of birth, death, and rebirth. It is the Jesus story.

The Exercise

1. Find your center and take three deep breaths.
2. With your next inhale, think "Jesus was born."
3. With your next exhale, think "Jesus died."
4. With your next inhale, think, "Jesus will come again."
5. Repeat steps 2-4 for most of the time you have given to your practice today.
6. When you are ready, release these. Sit in a time of wonder.

Day 18 The Visualization

Background: The next couple mind-clearing exercises-- the exercise for tomorrow and for day 24-- will rely on imagining ourselves at a riverside. I have found value in investing some time and head space into making this place as vital and vivid as is possible. Today, we will spend some time finding ourselves in that space.

The Exercise:

Find yourself at a calm riverside.

The temperature is your favorite here. Feel it on your skin. The soft breeze moves the cuff of your sleeves just a bit. Hear the gurgle of the river. It is just a few feet away. Water moves steadily over the rocks. Kneel in the dirt. Don't worry, you are wearing well-worn, well-loved pants ideal for this. Feel the refreshing chill of the water on your palms and fingers.

There is a place to sit. It is an old picnic bench. Or maybe a perfectly shaped rock. You could sit here, take your shoes off, and dangle your feet in the water if you wanted.

Look around. The sun filters green through the large leaves overhead. It is a beautiful forest, but there is one exceptional tree right here next to you. This tree? It has a personality. It's the sort of tree a person could talk to.

Look upriver. See a gentle curve in the there. There is a squirrel or rabbit scampering about. Perhaps a butterfly, too. And now, look downriver. The water froths a little more. There is an arrangement of rocks there, jutting up and out of the water. It's not really a dam. It's more of the sort of arrangement set up to make crossing the river easy. No jumping is required. Just careful placement of the feet from one boulder to the next. Along the riverbanks there is a group of large yellow flowers.

There are a few puffy clouds in an incredibly blue sky. It is quiet here. Was that the rat-a-tat of a woodpecker? Listen carefully. Perhaps it was.

Spend some time personalizing this place. It is yours. Fill it with your favorite animal or flower. Take a flight of fancy and make all the trees purple. Drink it in.

Explore this riverside area. Walk around. Find a path. Or a beautiful deer. There is a backpack hanging off your shoulder. Whatever you need is in there. Spend all the time you want enjoying this safe space. You can use it for the exercise we are doing tomorrow and next week. But it is also available for you whenever you want it. You can do spiritual practices here, or just come to wander around.

Day 19 Emptying the Mind.

Background: The novel 'Illusions: Adventures of the Reluctant Messiah' has an amazing scene. The protagonist is told to use the power of his mind to eliminate a group of clouds on the horizon. He spends the afternoon turning the whole of his will to the task. And he is thoroughly unsuccessful.

The man's mentor explains that he is entirely to emotionally wrapped up in the task to have ever been able to eliminate him. He would have done far better to withdraw his energies from the clouds than to invest himself.

This is a useful story. Sometimes, as we try to overcome our thoughts and feelings, we develop such an intensity that we will never be free from them. Imagining that we are at a riverside and seeing them all float by is a useful way to release these, to overcome our attachment to these distractions.

Spiritual Exercise

1. Breathe.

2. Return to the riverside setting you created yesterday. Remember to appeal to each of your senses: what is the temperature? What sounds do you hear? Can you note the texture of your clothes, or the feelings at your fingertips? What smells are being carried on the breeze?

3. As best you can, clear your mind. Continue to breathe in through your nose and out through your mouth.

4. Thoughts, feelings, and memories will arise. When they do, place them gently on the river. Allow them to be carried away.

5. Return to your breath.

Day 20: Apophatic Meditation

Background: These last several days; we have been focused on the tension between the "already happened" and the "not yet." One way to explore this through apophatic meditation is to consider a progression of events. Each might be considered in the present tense. We begin, for example, with the idea that "Jesus is being born." As usual, the affirmation is easy.

One of the meanings of "Jesus is not being born." is the obvious consideration that he is not now being born; this already happened. When we progress to the negation of the negation-- Jesus is *not* not being born, there is an element of affirming that Jesus' birth is an ongoing event, a thing that in some important way is still going on even now.

The Exercise

1. *Relax. Breathe deeply.*
2. *Inhale. Think, "Jesus is being born."*
3. *Exhale. Think, "Jesus is not being born."*
4. *Inhale. Think, "Jesus is not-not being born."*
5. *Exhale.*
6. *Inhale. Think, "Jesus is walking the earth with his disciples."*
7. *Exhale. Think, "Jesus is not walking the earth with his disciples."*
8. *Inhale. Think, "Jesus is not-not walking the earth with his disciples."*
9. *Exhale.*
10. *Inhale. Think, "Jesus is in the garden filled with doubt."*
11. *Exhale. Think, "Jesus is not in the garden filled with doubt."*
12. *Inhale. Think, "Jesus is not not in the garden filled with doubt."*
13. *Exhale.*
14. *Inhale. Think, "Jesus is betrayed at the last supper now."*
15. *Exhale. Think, "Jesus is not betrayed at the last supper now."*
16. *Inhale. Think, "Jesus is not not betrayed at the last supper now."*
17. *Exhale.*
18. *Inhale. Think, "Jesus walks among us again."*
19. *Exhale. Think, "Jesus does not walk among us again."*
20. *Inhale. Think "Jesus does not not walk among us again."*
21. *When you are ready, release this practice and sit in a time of wordless union.*

FIFTH GROUPING.

Our journey is a distant echo to a pair of events in the life of Jesus. He might have become tired and hungry and perhaps even bored as he moved in past the halfway point in the desert. To the extent these forty days measure his march to the cross, things begin to take a disturbing turn. Forces are gathering against him.

Perhaps things get dark and difficult here as you continue through these practices.

There are many wonderful and inspirational writers who have said many wonderful and inspirational things. Sometimes these words have helped me through difficult times. Other times they have made things more difficult on me. Perhaps you are the same.

In many of the most difficult things I have ever persevered through, I cannot attribute the fact that I made it through to the words of others. Though many have tried to tune me into them, I can't even say that the rather noble virtues like bravery and endurance were the ones that really inspired me. Sometimes, I have gotten through simply through bull-headed stubbornness. Of course, I do not know where you are on your journey through these 40 days and keeping up these practices... nor do I know where you are in the rest of your life.

But as I write these words, I am saying a prayer for you. My prayer is that you get what you need to hold on to that which you should be holding onto. I pray that if you need encouraging words you hear them; if calling on honorable courage will get you through that you find it; and if you are at the gut level of simply needing unthinking, blind, mechanical stubbornness, that you find this, too.

Day 21: Sacred Reading

Background: Today, we apply the first form of Lectio Divina that we did back in our very first exercise to a very different passage.

The Exercise:

1. *Release your worries and concerns for this time.*
2. *Take three deep breaths. With your exhalations, breathe out the things you think you know and the expectations you have on this time. With your inhalations, breathe in the Holy Spirit. Believe that you can hear from God.*
3. *Read the passage below. On the first read, just try to develop a general understanding of what is going on.*

Now when evening had come, he was reclining at the table with the twelve disciples. **21** As they were eating, he said, "Most certainly I tell you that one of you will betray me."

22 They were exceedingly sorrowful, and each began to ask him, "It isn't me, is it, Lord?"

23 He answered, "He who dipped his hand with me in the dish will betray me. **24** The Son of Man goes even as it is written of him, but woe to that man through whom the Son of Man is betrayed! It would be better for that man if he had not been born."

25 Judas, who betrayed him, answered, "It isn't me, is it, Rabbi?"

He said to him, "You said it."

26 As they were eating, Jesus took bread, gave thanks for[a] it, and broke it. He gave to the disciples and said, "Take, eat; this is my body." **27** He took the cup, gave thanks, and gave to them, saying, "All of you drink it, **28** for this is my blood of the new covenant, which is poured out for many for the remission of sins. **29** But I tell you that I will not drink of this fruit of the vine from now on, until that day when I drink it anew with you in my Father's Kingdom."

30 When they had sung a hymn, they went out to the Mount of Olives.

4. *Take three more deep breaths.*
5. *Now, read the passage above again. This time be awake and aware for details, portions, and elements that you are notice. Some think of this as a nudge from God. Others look for words and phrases that shine or sparkle. The important thing is simply being awake and aware for the sorts of things that come up for you.*
6. *Take three more deep breaths.*
7. *Read it through at least one more time, continuing to be open to whatever elements seem to stand out.*
8. *Take three more deep breaths.*
9. *Now, sit with the things that came up for you. Do not rush through the process of recalling the things you noticed today.*
10. *Take three more deep breaths.*
11. *When you are ready, begin to explore why these things might have come to your attention. Is there a common thread? Something that God might be speaking to you, now, through these words?*
12. *Take three more deep breaths. Release this practice. Sit in a time of wordless union.*
13. *If you wish, spend some time in prayer,*

thanking God for opening your eyes.

DAY 22 A BREATH PRAYER

It is said that St. Francis past an entire night asking 2 simple questions: "Who am I, God?" and "Who are you, God?" It is not known what his method was; the correlation of the two questions to the two parts of breath is purely speculation on my part.

The Exercise

1. *Sit up as straight as you comfortably can. Release your worries and obligations for the duration of your spiritual exercises today.*
2. *As you inhale, ask the question, "Who are you God?"*
3. *With your next inhale, ask the question, "Who am I God?"*
4. *Continue this pattern. When other thoughts or concerns arise, release them by returning to these questions and your breath.*
5. *When your time is nearing completion, dismiss the questions. Enjoy a time of wordless communion.*
6. *When you are ready, explore your feelings about the questions and consider whether you have anything that looks like answers to these two important questions.*

DAY 23:
VISUALIZATION-

Background: Today's visualization is a little bit different. It will not rely much on the sense of sight at all. This practice incorporates some elements of the group of practices known as mindfulness. One of the main characteristics of mindfulness is the idea that our senses do not have anxiety, fear, and regret. When we see, hear, touch, or taste we are in this particular moment, right here and now; not focused on the past or the future.

There are many mindful eating activities. These have been helpful in connecting people with their eating choices and helping them live in the moment. Today's practice takes this tradition and combines it with the wonderful and strange words of Jesus at the last supper. The food at that table was perhaps unique. It might be that the specially prepared wine, grape juice, crackers and bread served at specifically sanctioned religious rituals is important.

But this is not all that could or should be said on the matter. Father Richard Rohr said it powerfully, "The Eucharistic meal is meant to be a microcosmic event, summarizing at one table what is true in the whole macrocosm: We are one, we are equal in dignity, we all eat of the same divine food, and Jesus is still and always "eating with sinners" (for which people hated him) just as he did when on Earth." (This is from his wonderful daily email meditation, dated July 26, 2018)

In at least some sense, the idea that we eat of Jesus' body is connected to our connections with him. This is an assurance that just as we digest food and it becomes literally a part of us, so does Jesus. Jesus words are a promise that the universe has treasures to care for us and nourish us. He is everywhere.

Today's spiritual practice will be much more effective with something to eat. It does not need to be very much. A few small bites will do. In my experience, when I am eating mindfully, I tend to become aware of how much over processed, prepared, mass produced food is lacking. Therefore, a couple bits of apple might be much better than an entire microwave meal.

If it doesn't make sense to actually eat something with today's practice, then using the imagination to go through the steps is an alternate way to approach this.

The Exercise

1. *Take three deep breaths.*
2. *We will begin before eating the food to simply explore it. Entering this process with an open curiosity, as though you had never heard of this food will help.*
3. *Look at the food. Try and see it from a new angle.*
4. *If it is finger food, note the texture and temperature.*
5. *Recall Jesus' words, "This is my body." If you can, hear those words being said by him.*
6. *Take three deep breaths.*
7. *Smell the food.*
8. *Place a small bite of food in your mouth. Experience the texture and taste of this as it first goes in. Spend a moment with it in your mouth before you begin to bite down.*
9. *Recall Jesus; words, "This is my blood." If you can, hear those words being said by him.*
10. *Take three deep breaths.*
11. *Feel the texture of the food between your teeth. Enjoy how the process changes the food itself. The texture and flavor begin to shift.*
12. *As you continue to enjoy this food, recognize that Jesus is in this food. As you digest this food, Jesus will become even more one with you.*

Day 24: Clearing the Mind

It seems that there is some immutable center to us. This has been called the True Self. It can be the work of a lifetime to get past the things that seem like such an important part of who we are. Roles, titles, jobs, even callings... These are often good things. But they are not the most basic measure of who we are.

Today's Exercise

1. *Relax. Find your breath.*
2. *Return to the riverside location you created last week.*
3. *Furnish additional sensory information. What sounds are you hearing? What smells are you smelling? What is the temperature like? Are you sitting? What does your seat feel like?*
4. *Behold the river. See how the gentle current moves the water out of your vision.*
5. *Calm your mind. As thoughts enter your awareness, place them on the river. Allow the river to carry them out of your perceptions.*
6. *Continue to breathe deeply and slowly. As anything: feelings, memories, perception rise up to distract you from your breath, give them, gently to the river. Place them as you might put a leaf on the water, so gently to be sure it is floating in the cool water.*
7. *When you are ready, consider a trivial portion of your identity. Perhaps you are a football fan, or a lover of science fiction. Whatever that trivial aspect of your identity is, give it up to the river. Place it on the water and let the current carry it out of sight.*
8. *With your next breath, consider what it is like to be freed of this aspect of your identity.*
9. *Now, consider another aspect of your identity. Perhaps it is a certain distant familial relationship like uncle or cousin. Maybe it is a hobby you are very passionate about. Give this part of yourself to the river, now.*
10. *Experience life without this fact about yourself. Consider the ways you are changed. As distracting thoughts and feelings arise, remember to give these to the river, too.*
11. *Now, find something very important to you. Perhaps it is a job, a title, or a degree. Maybe it is your role within the family you live in (mother/ father/ sister/daughter, etc....) Give this role to the river as well.*
12. *Spend a breath experiencing yourself without this important role.*
13. *Consider that there is something within you. Explore who or what this is.*

14. *If it feels right, give additional aspects of your identity to the river.*

15. *You might even give your name itself to the river.*

16. *When you have given all the parts of yourself that you wish to, explore who you are, now. Consider your relationship with the divine. Think about what is left of you.*

17. *When you are ready, see yourself getting up from the riverside.*

18. *Walk downriver. Continue to not only see, but also hear and feel this world in your imagination. Perhaps fifty feet down the river, you will find that a number of rocks and branches lie across the river, obstructing the flow.*

19. *As you walk among these, you will find that many of the parts of yourself that you gave to the river sit here, prevented from going too far away. Consider each aspect of yourself. The ones you wish for, you can have back. Take them within you again. As for the ones you don't want? Untether them from the rocks and branches. Let them be washed free.*

Day 25: Apophatic Meditation

Background: One of the gifts of a contemplative stance is that it opens us up to the possibilities of nondualism. There are some statements which we overgeneralize from. For example, we might think all Republicans are bad. Or all Democrats are good. Or the reverse of those. In a case like this, if questioned about it, most of would generally agree that these statements are not true.

There are other times that we are faced with a paradox. Either there is an infinite list of things where each one created the next, or one thing simply *was* at the beginning of time. In this case, it appears that these are the only options. Yet both are absurd.

Apophatic meditation is a particularly good contemplative activity for developing this nondual stance. And nondualism? That might be the greatest of all the gifts of contemplative practice.

Today's practice is quite straightforward. There are only two statements. Sometimes, facing these contradictions head on is best, rather than allowing the focus to turn. It's worth noting that the timing of the exhales and the inhales is no accident. This configuration is meant to shift the sentences so that they are used equally on inhalations and exhalations.

The Exercise

1. *Release your stress and expectations on this time.*
2. *With the next inhale, think, "The bread is Jesus' body."*
3. *With the next exhale, think, "The bread is not Jesus' body."*
4. *With the next inhale, think, "The bread is not not Jesus' body."*
5. *Exhale.*
6. *Inhale.*
7. *With the next exhale, think, "The bread is Jesus' body."*
8. *With the next exhale, think, "The bread is not Jesus' body."*
9. *With the next inhale, think, "The bread is not not Jesus' body."*
10. *Exhale.*
11. *With the next inhale, think, "The wine is Jesus' blood."*
12. *With the next exhale, think, "The wine is not Jesus' blood."*
13. *With the next inhale, think, "The wine is not not Jesus' blood."*

14. *Exhale.*
15. *Inhale.*
16. *With the next exhale, think, "The wine is Jesus' blood."*
17. *With the next inhale, think, "The wine is not Jesus' blood."*
18. *With the next exhale, think, "The wine is not not Jesus' blood."*
19. *Repeat steps 2-18 as time permits.*
20. *Release this practice and sit in a time of wordless union.*

Sixth grouping

We are three quarters of the way through this journey.

If Jesus had stepped into the desert on the day you began your practice, he would be three-quarters of the way through his fast. If we looked at these days as a countdown to the cross, Jesus would be ten days away from death and resurrection.

I suppose in some ways you and I are both in the middle of a desert. And you and I are both also just a handful of days away from death and resurrection in our own lives. Can I invite you into a moment of reflection?

The desert is a hostile and unforgiving landscape. Food and water are the things which keep us going. What hostile landscapes are you traveling through? What sort of sustenance are you holding back from, whether by choice or necessity?

What sorts of death and resurrection are you walking toward?

If you have not begun to think about the next steps for your spiritual practice, I hope that you will begin to do so now. Over the long term, I do not recommend rotating between five different types of practice. As you work through these, I would encourage you to focus on 2 or 3 types of spiritual practice. I would do no more than 2 practices on a given day, for a total time of 30 minutes each day. Putting these practices on a regular rotation usually works well.

We are very lucky to have such huge options available to us. I hope the nature of this books makes my love of this variety clear.

It's worth naming this reality, though: for the vast history of spirituality, a huge number of people would have had access to a tiny number of practices. There are many ways that we are impoverished by the huge number of options that are available to us. There is wisdom in erring on the side of simplicity. So as you ponder your next steps and the shape of your spiritual practice, I hope that you will keep in mind the reality that one good practice is much better than splitting the time, attention, and head space between too many.

DAY 26: SACRED READING

Background: Today, we bring together our holy imagining practice from the second and fourth grouping. Recall that in the second we try to use our sensory information to enter the world of the narrative. On the fourth grouping we entered the narrative through the perspective of one of the figures that appeared in it. In that reading there was some mention of experiencing the narratives through the senses of that character. Today, we will be much more intentional and explicit about this goal.

The Exercise:
1. *Release your concerns. Take a deep breath.*
2. *Take three deep breaths. With each inhalation, breathe in the Holy Spirit. With each exhalation, breath out your preconceptions and expectations.*
3. *Read the following passage. On this first reading, simply try to get a grasp on the scope of the narrative.*

He came out and went, as his custom was, to the Mount of Olives. His disciples also followed him. 40 When he was at the place, he said to them, "Pray that you don't enter into temptation."

41 He was withdrawn from them about a stone's throw, and he knelt down and prayed, 42 saying, "Father, if you are willing, remove this cup from me. Nevertheless, not my will, but yours, be done."

43 An angel from heaven appeared to him, strengthening him. 44 Being in agony he prayed more earnestly. His sweat became like

great drops of blood falling on the ground.

45 When he rose up from his prayer, he came to the disciples, and found them sleeping because of grief, 46 and said to them, "Why do you sleep? Rise and pray that you may not enter into temptation."

47 While he was still speaking, a crowd appeared. He who was called Judas, one of the twelve, was leading them. He came near to Jesus to kiss him. 48 But Jesus said to him, "Judas, do you betray the Son of Man with a kiss?"

49 When those who were around him saw what was about to happen, they said to him, "Lord, shall we strike with the sword?" 50 A certain one of them struck the servant of the high priest, and cut off his right ear.

51 But Jesus answered, "Let me at least do this"—and he touched his ear and healed him. 52 Jesus said to the chief priests, captains of the temple, and elders, who had come against him, "Have you come out as against a robber, with swords and clubs? 53 When I was with you in the temple daily, you didn't stretch out your hands against me. But this is your hour, and the power of darkness."

4. *Re-read the passage above. This time be aware of the various perspectives you could experience this from. Be aware of a gentle tugging that might be a sense that you ought to experience this from that perspective. Recall that a figure does not need to be explicitly named.*

5. *Consider the perspective you have chosen. What is their personality? What is their mood? Hungry or happy? Tired or excited? Angry or joyful? Take three deep breaths. Put yourself in the mindset of this person.*

6. *Reread the passage slowly. See all the things that unfold through the eyes you have chosen. Experience them through the thoughts and feelings of this figure.*

7. *Read it one more time. This time experience the senses of that figure too. Imagine the texture of their clothing, the smell in the air, the sounds and the sights.*

8. *Spend some time reflecting on this passage and how it felt from this*

perspective.

DAY 27 BREATH PRAYER:

Background: This is one of those difficult places. There is nothing inherently wrong with the phrase, "Let not my will, but yours be done." But these words have been weaponized against some of us. As a result, today's breath prayer is presented in two different forms. The first uses most of the words we see in the scripture: "Not my will, but yours be done." The second might be better for those who are troubled by those words. In the second form of the breath prayer, the words will simply be, "Let your will be done." Even if you are comfortable with the first version, it is worth trying out the second. A breath prayer with no words on the inhale has a different character to it. As you move forward into building a spiritual practice beyond Lent, it is worth noticing these rather technical aspects of the spiritual exercises we are trying out so that when you create your own you have some experience with the ways that this practice can be done.

Exercise: Version 1
1. *Take 3 deep breaths as you release your worries and concerns.*
2. *With the next inhale, think "Not my will."*
3. *With your next exhale think, "Let your will be done."*
4. *Repeat steps 2 and 3 for most of the time you have devoted to your practice today.*
5. *When you are ready, release these words and sit in a time of wordless union.*

Exercise: Version 2

1. *Take 3 deep breaths as you release your worries and concerns.*
2. *Inhale.*
3. *With your exhale, think, "Let your will be done."*
4. *Repeat steps 2 and 3 for most of the time you have devoted to your practice today.*
5. *When you are ready, release these words and sit in a time of wordless union.*

DAY 28:
VISUALIZATION

Background: There have been times that everything you have wished for have seemed like they are to come to nothing. (And if you have never experienced this defeat, I offer you my deepest condolences. These defeats are important.)

Jesus' followers thought that everything was lost with his death. They watched his agonizing torture and they fled. They saw the enormous boulder rolled in front of his tomb. As you engage this visualization, I would like to challenge you to travel the space between experiencing this as one of his followers and holding your own disappointments. The disciples sat before this closed tomb and believed all the things they had hoped for were to come to nothing. Can you hold that thought for a moment as you entered this visualization: what if all the things you have hoped for are for nothing?

While it is generally not helpful to sit in abject misery, it is helpful to sit in unknowing. Most of us are not good in sitting in liminal spaces-- those between-times. As you watch this tomb, whether you look at it symbolically or within the narrative frame, do your best to put the eventual outcomes out of your mind. Spend this time in darkness and unknowing.

The Exercise:

See yourself. Close enough to look on the scene, not so close that anyone can connect you with your fallen teacher. His last words were correct. It is indeed finished. The air is not stirring enough to bring anything new and fresh. Even the bird cries sound mournful tonight.

Your eyes land on that enormous boulder. It is hard to imagine how even a well-coordinated detachment of Roman Soldiers might have gotten that in front of the opening into the side of the hill. A pair of Roman Soldiers flanks the door. It makes you angry that they look bored. Jesus was supposed to have changed everything.

Perhaps you can see the place where they crucified him from here. The sun is setting. You are thirsty and so, so tired. But you will sit here for a while yet. What else is there to do?

You might reflect on the best and the worst of times. The connections. The hope. You are too close to this to even begin to think about what will come next for you. For now, sit on the uncomfortable ground. Behold that tomb with the rock, the soldiers.

It is all gone.

DAY 29: EMPTYING THE MIND

Background: There are some states which are clearly contemplative. This mental state is much of the reason for trying a spiritual
practice in the first place. It's worth recognizing that spiritual
practices are not the only things which might get us there. Consider, for example, the act of watching the waves come in and
the beach. Even simply lying next to someone we love can bring
us there. Or recall a time you lay in the grass and watching the
clouds making an unhurried journey across a blue sky.

There are other states which are clearly not contemplative.
When we are focused on the fact that we are doing something we
don't want to do. When we are angry or viewing the world in a
dualistic either/ or sort-of way.

There is a vast landscape of states between these extremes.
That state of strange almost-hypnosis when riding in a car and the
streetlights are evenly spaced out. Losing ourselves in a moment
of flow during a game.

Today's mind clearing activity is to listen to music. This
activity is probably one which occupies that gray area between
the contemplative and the dualistic. But like many things, it is
much more about the attitude than the action that determines
whether something is contemplative.

It might be that the song you choose is one that has an explicit or implicit spirituality within by the lyrics. Perhaps it will
be specifically focused on Jesus' death and resurrection. This content is not at all necessary. In fact, the song does not even need to
have words.

There is an approach which can help this be more contemplative. In our everyday life, we can approach a song with an attitude of using the song as a means to an end. This end is relaxation, escape, or experiencing a certain emotion. In this context, if we think of something else that comes up for us during the song, it makes sense to follow this mental rabbit trail. One way to use music more contemplatively is to sink into the song, to slip further into it when potential distractions occur.

This is not the only contemplative approach to music. In the directions below I am not specifically mentioning the possibility for dance as a contemplative practice. This does not mean I don't think the practice isn't worth doing. Embodied practices like dance, yoga and drumming are incredibly powerful ones. I would deeply encourage you to explore these wonderful opportunities.

The Exercise
1. *Take three deep breaths to clear the mind.*
2. *Put the song on that you have chosen. Listen to it carefully.*
3. *As distractions arise, sink into the song. You might try to locate something in the song-- such as a specific instrument or a certain phrase, or even notes that are especially high or low-- and follow this through the whole song.*
4. *If you wish, sing with the song.*
5. *If you would like, repeat this process, with the same song or a different one.*

DAY 30: APOPHATIC MEDITATION

Background: As we enter the last quarter of our Lenten Journey, let's face the Easter mystery head on. In some impossible way, Jesus is on the cross. Also, he is in the tomb. Also, he has been resurrected. Each of these acts reverberates across space and time. Each is eternal in some sense.

This apophatic meditation is shorter than many in this book. It is good to go through it a few times. In an earlier apophatic meditation, we explored the idea that altering the negation of the negation sometimes helps to create a balance. This way there is an equal number of statements associated with an inhale and an exhale.

At this time, we practiced an apophatic meditation while holding the breath with the third statement. In today's practice, we split the negation of the negation between an inhale and exhale. This is tricky to time well. Fortunately, it is not critical that it is timed well. The danger of this method is getting overly concerned with starting the negation of the negation at precisely the right time. However, it works out will be fine.

The Exercise
   1. *Relax and release your concerns and worries.*
   2. *With your next inhale, think "Jesus is on the cross."*
   3. *With your next exhale, think "Jesus is not on the cross."*
   4. *Exhale. Think, "Jesus is on the cross"*
   5. *Inhale. Think "not in the cross."*
   6. *Inhale. Exhale.*

7. *With your next inhale, think "Jesus is in his tomb."*

8. *With your next exhale, think "Jesus is not in his tomb."*

9. *Exhale. Think, "Jesus is not-"*

10. *Inhale. Think "not in his tomb."*

11. *Inhale. Exhale.*

12. *With your next inhale, think "Jesus walks on the Earth."*

13. *With your next exhale, think "Jesus does not walk on the Earth."*

14. *Exhale. Think, "Jesus does not--"*

15. *Inhale. Think "not walk on the Earth."*

16. *Inhale. Exhale.*

17. *With your next inhale, think "Jesus is in Heaven"*

18. *With your next exhale, think "Jesus is not in Heaven"*

19. *Exhale. Think, "Jesus is not--"*

20. *Inhale. Think "not in Heaven."*

21. *Repeat these statements, as you have time.*

SEVENTH GROUPING

In terms of our journey toward Easter, let this be the darkest time.

In terms of building a spiritual practice, each of our five practices will be practiced two more times. By now, you probably have a good sense of which practices come easily and which do not. There is value in all the practices. As you continue to consider which ones to incorporate into your spiritual practice beyond these 40 days, I hope you can take a view of your spiritual practice like the view we take toward the things we put in our body.

Like many people, I love carbs. Pretzels. Pizza. Pasta. Give it all to me. If I knew nothing about nutrition, I would probably try to eat nothing but carbs. Of course, if I never had any fruits or vegetables, if I never sought out proteins, I would have a few problems.

The point is that sometimes I eat the things which are not my favorite things. The things that I don't like are sometimes the things I need to eat the most. And it is the same with our spiritual "dietary" needs. It might be that the practice you resist the most is also the practice you need the most.

This, of course, can be overdone. If you build a spiritual practice exclusively around those practices which are the most difficult there are two possible results. One is that you give up. The second is that you are miserable. Neither of these is a good outcome.

The bottom line here is that a balance ought to be struck. Now is the time to begin to think about what that balance might look like.

DAY 31: SACRED READING

Background: Today we return to *Lectio Divina.* We have done two different forms of this practice with two different passages from the bible. First, we engaged in a form of this practice which invited us to find a phase we turned into a breath prayer. Then, we entered the passage with an openness to whatever sections we might be called to notice. This second version is a little more open than the first.

Today the passage we read will be the crucifixion. The approach we take to *Lectio* will be like the second approach. The idea continues to be that we are looking for God to speak to us in a general way and are not assuming that this will be in a verse that is easy to turn into a breath prayer.

The difference is that this time we will begin with a bit of a self-assessment. By beginning this way, we recall specific issues God can help us with or even specific questions that God might answer. In my experience, the good news about this variation is that it tends to focus the practice on the ideas I notice in the self-assessment. Also, the bad news is that this variation tends to focus the practice on the ideas I noticed in the self-assessment.

A warning is in order here. This should not be the be-all and end-all of discernment. This practice is a helpful way to generate a bit of helpfulness. It would be unwise, in most circumstances, to base an important decision on a single use of *Lectio Divina.*

The Exercise
   1. Take three deep breaths.

2. *Over these next several minutes take a mental account of where we are in various aspects of where you are. With the next inhale, consider your work or school situation. Spend whatever time you need to think about what is going well about this aspect of your life, and what is going poorly.*

3. *Inhale. Exhale your thoughts about work and school.*

4. *Inhale and exhale again.*

5. *With the next inhale, consider your relationships. Think about family and friends. Spend whatever time you need to think about what is going well about this aspect of your life, and what is going poorly.*

6. *Inhale. Exhale your thoughts about relationships.*

7. *Inhale and exhale again.*

8. *With the next inhale, consider your physical, mental, and spiritual health. Spend whatever time you need to think about what is going well about this aspect of your life, and what is going poorly.*

9. *Inhale. Exhale your thoughts about health.*

10. *Inhale and exhale again.*

11. *Put these thoughts together. Choose a single area (or two) that you would like illuminated by todays practice. This might be in the form of a question. It might be a bit broader than that. It would be very wise to write this down somewhere in case you lose track of it in your mind. Express this as a prayer for clarity, answers, support, or whatever it is that you need.*

12. *Read the following passage. On this first read through, just read it for basic understanding of what is going to happen.*

As they came out, they found a man of Cyrene, Simon by name, and they compelled him to go with them, that he might carry his cross. 33 When they came to a place called "Golgotha", that is to say, "The place of a skull," 34 they gave him sour wine[b] to drink mixed with gall.[c] When he had tasted it, he would not drink. 35 When they had crucified him, they divided his clothing among them, casting lots,[d] 36 and they sat and watched him there. 37 They set up over his head the accusation against him written, "THIS IS JESUS, THE KING OF THE JEWS."

38 Then there were two robbers crucified with him, one on his right hand and one on the left.

39 Those who passed by blasphemed him, wagging their heads 40 and saying, "You who destroy the temple and build it in three days, save yourself! If you are the Son of God, come down from the cross!"

41 Likewise the chief priests also mocking with the scribes, the Phari-sees,[e] and the elders, said, 42 "He saved others, but he can't save him-self. If he is the King of Israel, let him come down from the cross now, and we will believe in him. 43 He trusts in God. Let God deliver him now, if he wants him; for he said, 'I am the Son of God.'" 44 The robbers also who were crucified with him cast on him the same reproach.

45 Now from the sixth hour[f] there was darkness over all the land until the ninth hour.[g] 46 About the ninth hour Jesus cried with a loud voice, saying, "Eli, Eli, lima[h] sabachthani?" That is, "My God, my God, why have you forsaken me?" Psalm 22:1

47 Some of them who stood there, when they heard it, said, "This man is calling Elijah."

48 Immediately one of them ran and took a sponge, filled it with vinegar, put it on a reed, and gave him a drink. 49 The rest said, "Let him be. Let's see whether Elijah comes to save him."

50 Jesus cried again with a loud voice, and yielded up his spirit.

51 Behold, the veil of the temple was torn in two from the top to the bottom. The earth quaked and the rocks were split. 52 The tombs were opened, and many bodies of the saints who had fallen asleep were raised; 53 and coming out of the tombs after his resurrection, they en-tered into the holy city and appeared to many.

54 Now the centurion and those who were with him watching Jesus, when they saw the earthquake and the things that were done, were ter-rified, saying, "Truly this was the Son of God!"

55 Many women were there watching from afar, who had followed

Jesus from Galilee, serving him. 56 *Among them were Mary Magdalene, Mary the mother of James and Joses, and the mother of the sons of Zebedee.*

57 *When evening had come, a rich man from Arimathaea named Joseph, who himself was also Jesus' disciple, came.* 58 *This man went to Pilate and asked for Jesus' body. Then Pilate commanded the body to be given up.* 59 *Joseph took the body and wrapped it in a clean linen cloth* 60 *and laid it in his own new tomb, which he had cut out in the rock. Then he rolled a large stone against the door of the tomb, and departed.* 61 *Mary Magdalene was there, and the other Mary, sitting opposite the tomb.*

62 *Now on the next day, which was the day after the Preparation Day, the chief priests and the Pharisees were gathered together to Pilate,* 63 *saying, "Sir, we remember what that deceiver said while he was still alive: 'After three days I will rise again.'* 64 *Command therefore that the tomb be made secure until the third day, lest perhaps his disciples come at night and steal him away, and tell the people, 'He is risen from the dead;' and the last deception will be worse than the first."*

65 *Pilate said to them, "You have a guard. Go, make it as secure as you can."* 66 *So they went with the guard and made the tomb secure, sealing the stone.*

13. *Inhale. Exhale.*
14. *Remind yourself-- or reread-- the concerns you were bringing to your practice today.*
15. *Reread the passage above. Look through the lens of this question or aspect of your life. Pay attention to your body and keep your concern in your mind as best you can. It is not necessary to understand why a certain passage impacts you. Simply be present to this.*
16. *Inhale. Exhale. If nothing came up for you, read the passage a third time.*
17. *Sit in a time of contemplation around the words that came up for you. Do you have a sense of what they mean and how they relate to your concerns?*

18. *If you would like, read through the passage a final time. Explore whether you have a new understanding and appreciation of your situation or this passage.*

19. *Thank God for the work he did with and in you today.*

DAY 32: BREATH PRAYER

Background: The Eastern (Orthodox) churches have a long history of supporting the repetition of this phrase. It is traditionally suggested that this be said from the "heart" and not the "head." The instructions are generally to say it without ceasing, preferably out loud. The goal is to reach a place of ceaseless prayer, where these words are constantly being thought and experienced.

The Exercise

1. *Place your feet flat on the floor.*
2. *Breathe in through your nose, and out through your mouth.*
3. *Say the following words out loud. Try to feel their meaning. "Lord Jesus Christ, son of God, have mercy on me, a sinner."*
4. *Repeat that phrase for the duration of your spiritual practice.*

DAY 33 VISUALIZATION

Background: This is a time of being open to mystery and suffering. That is no easy thing.

We all have different ways we wish to retreat from these. After much suffering, we begin to realize that the retreat causes many more problems than the pain. Left to my own devices, when I am told to stop running from pain my temptation is to go to the opposite extreme, rather than retreat from pain I wallow in it. There is some broken, masochistic side of me that almost seems to enjoy it.

I am learning that my body is sometimes wiser than my mind. One way I can find middle ground between retreat and wallowing is taking ownership of my physical sensations. There are many parts of me that report on where I am without dwelling on these things. Today's visualization is quite different from the past visualizations we have engaged in. Rather than transporting us somewhere new and different, lets lean deeply into where we are right now.

The body scan is a well-loved mindfulness exercise. This is a practice which invites us to carefully survey the body and to explore how it is feeling. One of the objectives is to compare how the different body parts feel. Those parts of us that feel relaxed are contrasted with the places we feel tense.

It's a powerful thing, to note what feels comfortable. Just as watching the example of someone performing well is often more helpful than analyzing what is wrong, finding parts of the body which are comfortable allows us to use them as a sort of example in how to bring that comfort elsewhere.

On this approach, the soreness is simply noted. Noticing has a strange kind of power in contemplation. Sometimes, just the act of no-ticing is enough to make the situation feel better. It is a bit like putting a band aid on the "owie" of a small child.

The exercise that is on the next page is written with this simple approach of merely noticing. After you feel comfortable with this, you might try the following variations and see how they work for you. These variations bring a more active focus to the places which do not feel com-fortable.

The first variation is to "breathe into" the hurt. As we inhale, we imagine the breath going straight to the place that is sore. Envisioning the breath coming to work on the painful place can be very effective.

The second variation is to turn the attention to relaxing the area. Here, we will the muscles themselves to relax. Sometimes it is helpful to begin with the surrounding area and work our way inward, toward the center of the discomfort.

After a particularly good body scan, I become delightfully aware of the ways my body parts are all connected. I notice the joints, ligaments, and places that connect one part of me to another. I get this sense of being a single, unified body rather than just a collection of parts.

The Exercise

1. *Inhale.*
2. *Exhale.*
3. *Inhale again and turn the attention to the soles of both feet. Explore them front to back or left to right. Let yourself be-come aware of where they are and how they are feeling.*
4. *Now, draw your attention up through the tops of the feet.*
5. *Become aware of the ankles and lower calves. Continue to be aware of how these body parts are feeling.*
6. *In your mind's eye, see your shins, too.*
7. *Become aware of the knees, and the area behind the knees. Continue to draw the attention up to the thighs.*
8. *Remembering to continue to breathe deeply, now notice the*

pelvis, hips, and buttocks.

9. *Bring your awareness to your lower back and abdomen.*
10. *Draw your attention up, through the rib cage and shoulders.*
11. *Inhale. Exhale.*
12. *Wiggle your fingers. Bring your awareness to each finger and thumb. Notice where they come to join the hand.*
13. *Feel your palm and notice the back of your hand.*
14. *Continuing to breathe deeply, note your wrist and forearms.*
15. *Draw your attention to the elbow and upper arm.*
16. *Note your armpit and the place where your arm joins the body.*
17. *Inhale. Exhale.*
18. *Turn your attention to everything below the neck. You have become aware of that whole portion of your body.*
19. *Now, draw your awareness up the neck.*
20. *Become aware of the jaw, and slowly draw your attention across your face. Feel how your nose and ear sit in your skull. Become mindful of how your eyes and sinuses feel.*
21. *Notice the back of your head, and slowly draw your awareness up through the very top of the scalp.*
22. *Now, relax for a few minutes, enjoying the connection with your body.*

DAY 34: CLEARING THE MIND

Background: If you wanted to divide up all the spiritual exercises, all the contemplations, all the ways of approaching of mindfulness that have ever been, you could find one convenient dividing line around what they do with the breath.

Many practices begin by asking us to take charge of the breath. Generally speaking, these practices encourage us to slow down our breathing. There are lots of reasons that this is a good idea.

As discussed above, it may not be the most accurate picture of the way things work though.

The other category of practices asks us to simply observe the breath.

The act of simply tuning into the breath can be so much more difficult than it sounds. It is easy to overthink the direction, "Tune into your breath without changing it." Generally speaking, holding this instruction to tightly will lead to struggles. In trying to be too literal we tend to unleash a series of questions and doubts.

As with so many things, entering these exercises in a light-hearted manner is wise. If we accept that we will not be perfect at it, we will be able to observe our breath much more effectively.

The Exercise:

1. *Sit in a comfortable, upright manner if you are able.*
2. *Tune in to your breath. Do your best to accept it without changing it.*
3. *Note whether you are using the mouth, nose, or both.*
4. *Become aware of specifically where you feel the breath entering the nose or mouth. How does it feel there? What is the temperature?*

5.   *Note the temperature as it comes in.*
6.   *Extend this awareness of the feeling and temperature as the breath leaves you.*
7.   *Where does the breath end in your body? Does your abdomen move? Your chest?*
8.   *When you are ready, increasingly bring yourself into this breath. The one you feel right now. This breath now is the only breath you can ever change. It is wholly unique among all the breaths you will ever feel. Greet each breath. Find its uniqueness.*
9.   *Welcome the special breaths that follow in the same way. Sit in this awareness for most of the time you have devoted to your practice today.*
10.   *When you are ready, return to your everyday life. But know that you can welcome each breath throughout your day.*

DAY 35: APOPHATIC MEDITATION

Background: As we finish up this bleak five days, we enter a somber and straight forward apophatic meditation. Rather than stringing together an entire a group of phrases, it can be a powerful thing to simply home in on one. This is what we will do today for our final two apophatic meditations.

This time we will modify our order a bit. Rather than progress through all three phrases at once we will repeat the affirmation three times, the negation three times, and the negation of the negation three times. If this seems confusing, don't worry. It will fall together in the description.

The Exercise

1. *Take three deep breaths.*
2. *With the next inhale, think, "Jesus is dead."*
3. *With the next exhale, think, "Jesus is dead."*
4. *With the next inhale, think, "Jesus is dead."*
5. *Exhale.*
6. *Take another deep breath.*
7. *With the next inhale, think "Jesus is not dead."*
8. *With the next exhale, think, "Jesus is not dead."*
9. *With the next inhale, think, "Jesus is not dead."*
10. *Exhale.*
11. *Take another deep breath.*
12. *With the next inhale, think, "Jesus is not-not dead."*
13. *With the next exhale, think, "Jesus is not-not dead."*
14. *With the next inhale, think "Jesus is not-not dead."*
15. *Exhale.*
16. *Take another deep breath.*
17. *As time permits, repeat steps 2-16.*

EIGHTH GROUPING

And the journey ends, now.

This is a time of joy. But let's not let this joy come too cheaply. The fact that Jesus is alive justifies his suffering and death. And yet it does not erase it. Holding onto the darkness helps us to fully appreciate the light.

DAY 36: SACRED READING

Our last sacred reading exercise will be a holy imagining practice. This is a different passage than we have used previously. It is a similar practice, though.

The Exercise:
1. *Release your concerns. Take a deep breath.*
2. *Take three deep breaths. With each inhalation, breathe in the Holy Spirit. With each exhalation, breath out your preconceptions and expectations.*
3. *Read the following passage. On this first reading, simply try to get a grasp on the scope of the narrative.*

Now after the Sabbath, as it began to dawn on the first day of the week, Mary Magdalene and the other Mary came to see the tomb. 2 Behold, there was a great earthquake, for an angel of the Lord descended from the sky and came and rolled away the stone from the door and sat on it. 3 His appearance was like lightning, and his clothing white as snow. 4 For fear of him, the guards shook, and became like dead men. 5 The angel answered the women, "Don't be afraid, for I know that you seek Jesus, who has been crucified. 6 He is not here, for he has risen, just like he said. Come, see the place where the Lord was lying. 7 Go quickly and tell his disciples, 'He has risen from the dead, and behold, he goes before you into Galilee; there you will see him.' Behold, I have told you."

8 They departed quickly from the tomb with fear and great joy, and ran to bring his disciples word. 9 As they went to tell his disciples, behold, Jesus met them, saying, "Rejoice!"

They came and took hold of his feet, and worshiped him.

10 Then Jesus said to them, "Don't be afraid. Go tell my brothers [a] that they should go into Galilee, and there they will see me."

11 Now while they were going, behold, some of the guards came into the city and told the chief priests all the things that had happened. 12 When they were assembled with the elders and had taken counsel, they gave a large amount of silver to the soldiers, 13 saying, "Say that his disciples came by night and stole him away while we slept. 14 If this comes to the governor's ears, we will persuade him and make you free of worry." 15 So they took the money and did as they were told. This saying was spread abroad among the Jews, and continues until today.

16 But the eleven disciples went into Galilee, to the mountain where Jesus had sent them. 17 When they saw him, they bowed down to him; but some doubted. 18 Jesus came to them and spoke to them, saying, "All authority has been given to me in heaven and on earth. 19 Go[b] and make disciples of all nations, baptizing them in the name of the Father and of the Son and of the Holy Spirit, 20 teaching them to observe all things that I commanded you. Behold, I am with you always, even to the end of the age." Amen.

> 9. Re-read the passage above. This time, be aware of the various perspectives you could experience this from. Be aware of a gentle tugging that might be a sense that you ought to experience this from that perspective. Recall that a figure does not need to be explicitly named.
>
> 10.　　　　Consider the perspective you have chosen. What

is their personality? What is their mood? Hungry or happy? Tired or excited? Angry or joyful? Take three deep breaths. Put yourself in the mindset of this person.

11.   *Reread the passage slowly. See all the things that unfold through the eyes you have chosen. Experience them through the thoughts and feelings of this figure.*

12.   *Read it one more time. This time experience the senses of that figure too. Imagine the texture of their clothing, the smell in the air, the sounds and the sights.*

13.   *Spend some time reflecting on this passage and how it felt from this perspective.*

DAY 37: BREATH PRAYER

Background: Mainstream, liturgical churches have a well-loved call-and-response. One person says, "he is risen." The congregation replies, "he is risen indeed."

It seems like a simple thing. For some of us it is so common that it can escape our notice that there is something wonderful happening in this exchange. After the doubt and the darkness of Jesus' death, we begin with a statement that is great news. Someone tell us that Jesus is resurrected. After our time of doubt —which was an important experience—we now move into the light. We affirm this great news. But we don't merely repeat something back that has already been said. We add a little tiny word. And with those two little syllables, we go further than merely affirming.

There are many things we could have said which misuse language, but which would make a similar point. The heart knows what we mean if we replied, "Yes, he is very much risen." Or "He is extremely risen." But those words aren't quite right. On a literal level they are wrong even if there is some poetic traction there.

Though the word 'indeed' is a little bit dated, it is a powerful word here. And, of course, it is used correctly. There aren't any better ways to convey this idea. That word has a way of implying something like, "I want to go beyond simply agreeing with your point. I want to highlight it, I want it make it bold-faced, if I had words to make it more intensely, I would."

The Exercise

1. *Inhale. Exhale. Repeat three times.*

2. *With the next inhale, think "He is risen."*

3. *With the exhale, think "He is risen indeed."*

4. *Repeat steps 3 and 4 for most of the time you had planned for today.*

DAY 38:
VISUALIZATION

Background: If you had asked me, several years ago, I would have told you I was quite comfortable with recognizing that God is equal parts male and female. In my head, I became quite comfortable with this idea quite some time ago.

The first time I really felt at home in a church pastored by a woman, I realized I wasn't quite there yet. The experience was surprising to me on a few different levels. I also would have thought I did not do a whole lot of projection about God's nature based on the characteristics of the pastor who lead my church. I would have been wrong there, too, though.

While connecting at the church, I began to grow. I realized that I paid lip service to a nongendered God, I wasn't quite there yet. But having a female pastor made this easier for me.

Visualizations like this one are good for me. Perhaps they are for you, too. They force me to face the fact that God is both woman and man. This visualization is particularly appropriate for the end of a Lenten exploration.

The idea of spending 3 days dead in the Earth is a strange one. It is full of darkness and mystery. But there is a womb-like element to all of this, too. One layer of meaning around the idea that a beaten, broken, dead Jesus was placed in the tomb is that he was returning to God's womb to be healed and reborn.

The exercise

1. *Close your eyes. Sit in a comfortable position.*

2. *Take 3 deep breaths. Try to fully empty your lungs with the exhales*

and fully inflate your lungs with the inhales.

3. Imagine yourself dwelling in the womb of God. It is a place that is safe, comfortable, and warm.

4. Feel all your needs for food and oxygen being met through a cord that reaches into your body through your navel. Know that you are protected in this place.

5. Continue those deep breaths. Luxuriate in the way you are being nourished and prepared for what is next.

6. Take all the time that you need.

7. God is within you. Know that this is true. Take a deep breath.

8. Live in the paradox that even as you are in God, God is in you.

9. God may be small, now. But a divine spark is within. See this spark as a child in a womb.

10. Know that you are nourishing this God-spark. It is growing strong and healthy in the dark mystery within you.

11. As you continue to breathe deeply and hold to the image that you are in God's womb, cultivate this idea that God is also in your womb.

12. Sit in this comfortable paradox, this warm, nourishing safe reality for as long as you need, today.

DAY 39: CLEARING THE MIND

Background: It would be difficult to find an item more commonly used than a candle for ritual and contemplative practices. There are many who have used it as a symbol of the divine or human consciousness.

The subtle movement of a candle is a sort-of visual equivalent to a mantra, a thing just busy enough to occupy the mind to allow us to release everything else.

As we celebrate Jesus' resurrection this candle can be more. Jesus is quite frequently referred to as a light, particularly in the gospel of John. The lighting of the candle can be experienced as a symbol for his sudden return into the world. I recommend strongly that before you begin this practice that you get everything ready. Have the candle waiting somewhere safe. Ideally it would be a few feet away, directly in the sight line of wherever you will be doing this practice from. Also be ready with matches or lighter.

The Practice
1. *Take three deep breaths.*
2. *As you light the candle, declare this flame a symbol of Jesus' return from death.*
3. *Inhale. Exhale.*
4. *Let your eyes land on the flame. Seek to empty your mind.*
5. *When distractions arise, return your view to the flame.*

DAY 40: APOPHATIC MEDITATION

Background: There are many ideas about what Jesus death and resurrection mean. There is probably some element of truth in each. There is also falsehood within each picture as well. No matter how powerful your own words for what this action mean, they also fall short. You might wish to add your own beliefs about the meaning of Jesus' death, if it is not mentioned her.

The Exercise
1. *Take 3 deep breaths.*
2. *With your next inhale, think "Jesus died to atone for my sins."*
3. *With your next exhale, think, "Jesus did not die to atone for my sins."*
4. *With your next inhale, think, "Jesus did not not die to atone for my sins."*
5. *Exhale.*
6. *Inhale.*
7. *Exhale.*
8. *With your next inhale, think, "Jesus died to show God's love."*
9. *With your next exhale, think, "Jesus did not die to show God's love."*
10. *With your next inhale, think "Jesus did not not die to show God's love."*
11. *Exhale.*
12. *Inhale.*

13. *Exhale.*
14. *With your next inhale, think "Jesus died to stop the cycle of violence."*
15. *With your next exhale, think, "Jesus did not die to stop the cycle of violence."*
16. *With your next inhale, think, "Jesus did not not die to stop the cycle of violence."*
17. *Exhale.*
18. *Inhale.*
19. *Exhale.*
20. *Repeat steps 2-19, as time permits.*
21. *Release these words. Sit in a time of wordless union.*

AFTERWORD

My hope, as you have read these words and engaged these practices, is that you have indeed been set afire. Along the way, I hope that you realized, with St. John of the Cross, that you are a candle. Combusting only seems like a bad plan if you were not made to do so in the first place. A candle that never knows fire seems like something that has missed out on its deepest calling.

I have spent some time sitting with this imagery: the idea that I might be a candle.

One of my first reactions was to wonder about what happens when the candle is through. When the wick has run its course, it seems as though there is nothing left. There is a part of this disturbing image that resonates. When I feel God's presence in my deepest places, there is a sense that this process is ruining me for so much of what I see in the world.

But... when I reflect more deeply, I discover that the things I am being ruined for were never very good for me in the first place. When I experience God's presence I am suddenly less interested in shallow conversations, reality television, pursuits after money or power for the sake of money of power and fast food hamburgers. These things were never good for me in the first place.

God's presence in me reminds me of my worth. When it happens.

It does not always happen. I have gone days, weeks, months, and years without feeling lit on fire. There are seasons of my life where I feel like a candle that is sitting on a shelf gathering dust. Lent has lessons in this. Forty days in the desert. Betrayal, torture, and three days dead. This is such an important part of the process.

When I went away to the retreat I expected to play with

those metaphorical sparklers. When I look at the way Easter is recognized, I see it as more of the same: just toying around with pretty lights. This is largely because of the ways we deny that darkness. We pretend that resurrection is possible without dying in the first place.

A candle is most useful in the darkness. If there was always a noon time sun, we would not need them at all. When I think about a candle that appears as though it's time is gone, when I really meditate on a little pile of melted wax with the ashy remnants of a wick sitting in it, I realize it is only telling half the story to say that the thing is gone.

Really, the candle was transformed!

It was transformed into hope and light. That hope and light filled up not only the air around it. It also penetrated the people whose way it lit. It changed them by illuminating the words they read which entered their brain. It heartened them by allowing for hope and community around a kitchen table where the darkness was dispelled for a little while.

By the time the candle has burned itself out, there is a sense in which the light is gone. But only one sense. Whatever joy or freedom or understanding that light brought is now a part of the whole universe. After we are lit on fire, there is a part of us that is consumed. And a part of us that is set free. This is our final destination.

Before I started down this path, back in my time or believing that most of the power of Christ could be conveyed through a 40 minute sermon, back when I thought that the measure of a Christian was in their compliance to doctrines that can be expressed with words, I would have expected a writer to continue to explain this metaphor.

I am after all, talking about God's kingdom here. I am talking about heaven and our final destination. At that time, I would have expected that someone could read the bible very carefully and then convey what it all means. The reality is that I have no idea just what all this means. I don't know what heaven or hell will be like in their specifics. I have no words to express how it is likely to go.

I have had these practices, though. Meditations on life and death. Experiences of God's presence and Gods absences. And these? They are enough and more than enough.

APPENDIX ON FASTING

Lent has been associated with fasting for hundreds of years. It seems that one of the reasons for this is a desire to be cued into an awareness of Jesus' suffering. Sometimes, this is a good thing. I grow increasingly convinced that there are very few things that can be judged based only on the external specifics of the action itself. Almost always, if I want to know whether something seems right or wrong, I am interested in knowing the motivations of those involved.

(It ought to be noted that the to discern the wisdom and strategic value of a decision the case is quite the opposite. When it comes to whether something is tactically wise, the intent of the people involved seems quite irrelevant.)

Most of us would agree that the mentality that leads to fasting can be taken too far when we look at the practices from past centuries. Christians have whipped and crucified themselves in an attempt to understand Jesus' suffering. Hopefully most of us agree that this is a bad idea.

I am, of course, much less noble and wise than Jesus. But during those times when I have suffered, I have never wanted my loved ones to literally recreate my own suffering. To bring this down to the small and mundane. If I stub my toe, I am not interested in my wife taking off her shoes and kicking the bed corner, too.

Clearly, there is some sort of limits to the wisdom of wanting to share in Jesus suffering.

There are tendencies within the church that make this

extra challenging. There is a history of emphasizing the exile from the Garden of Eden and downplaying the fact that we were made in God's image, breathed into by God Godself.

When we have received and internalized too many messages about our sinfulness, our unworthiness, our unsuitability, the very concept of a fast can grow perverted. The suggestion that we ought to give something up at Lent can follow a thought process that looks something like this:

I am bad. I deserve to be punished. What's that? A season is coming up when people abstain from things they would normally allow themselves? Sign me up! That is what I deserve in the first place!

This, of course, is exactly the wrong spirit to approach a fast from. There is a mindset which on the surface looks quite similar. This resemblance is only skin deep, though. This is a much healthier perspective to approach a fast from.

There is a critical distinction between feeling that we deserve pain and knowing that we can withstand pain. This is where a healthier approach to a fast begins.

It might mean a lot more than this, but at the bare minimum, the lesson of Lent is this: deaths will happen. Resurrections will occur.

There is the most obvious and specific death that will occur at the end of our lives. But there are also little deaths along the way. We do not see the life that will spring up on the other side of these deaths, often. Our natural inclination is to run from them.

There is something Jesus-like in the act of facing these little deaths head on. One way to do this is to abstain from something we would normally participate in. This is a tiny echo of Jesus' choice to die on the cross. Growth can arise from this decision.

Sadly, it does not seem like merely reading and thinking about this is enough to change it. The thing I am trying to say here is that there are many people who would not benefit from a fast through lent. I would go so far as to say that unless you are feeling quite convinced that a fast is a good and healthy thing to do, you ought to abstain. Call it a fast from fasting if you would like.

If you feel that a fast is a wise decision, we then find ourselves wondering what that fast is going to look like. Let's begin with the observation that it is remarkable how much we have complicated our lives. We spend so much time so far removed from the things we really need. And yet, we tell ourselves we need it all. The reality is that even the things we do need, we do not need them with the same urgency and in the same amounts that we might begin to believe we do.

It is profoundly unnatural to do without. The parts of us that seek out the things we need or the things we think we need make their attempt at running the show. They can take over everything if we are not careful.

Resisting this desire helps us to see the difference between the things we need and the things we think we need. It shows us that we might not have needed them in the first place. It resists the temptation to let our appetites run the show. We prove to ourselves that we are bigger than our desire for this thing or that thing.

When we are not spending money, time, or headspace on things that we usually do we find that these resources are suddenly freed up for something else. This is one of the magical aspects of fasting. When we can incorporate into the fast a plan to reuse these now freed up resources elsewhere, that is where magic happens. If we are fasting from something that costs money, we might give that money to a worthy cause. If we are fasting from something that normally wastes time, we might dedicate that time to something more worthy.

This all becomes easier to explore when we make it a little bit more specific. Let's begin with the most obvious choice: food.

Some people abstain entirely from eating for a certain period. There are negatives and positives to this. Please see a medical professional before fasting from food and please continue to hydrate yourself. Drinking water very regularly is important.

Even if we have made the decision to abstain from solid foods for a certain time there are still several things to consider. One is the presence of caffeine. If your body expects your morning cup of coffee, will you deprive it this along with sustenance? Will you allow yourself juice? The brief times I have abstained from food I have found a few things.

One of them is that I can be quite pathetic and whiny.

Another is that leaning into God during difficult times works. When I make the conscious decision that I will turn each stomach growl into an opportunity to think about God, I find that I quite enjoy the opportunity to be so very connected.

The time and money that would have been spent on meal prep and food can be leveraged for some other purpose when we are fasting from food. And, of course, it is not necessary to abstain from all food.

American Catholics quite famously abstain from red meat on Fridays through Lent. This practice ends up being a rather helpful one. Many experts on the environment suggest that eating meat is a major cause of environmental problems. Though it is difficult for many of us (including your author!) to make the transition away from meat entirely, reducing the red meat we consume is a wonderful first step.

If we decide that we are going to fast from some foods, we don't of course have to focus only on meat. We might focus on some sort of unnecessary splurge like our expensive morning coffee, the cookies we eat, or the alcohol we drink.

Fasts of this type are helpful because they turn our attention to how utterly extravagant many of our food choices are. It's natural to rationalize that we biologically must eat. But in fact, most of us go well above and beyond the bare minimum.

Of course, we don't have to focus on food at all. We can try and fast from activities like social media, screen time, movies, or the like. We might notice that we tend to swear often and decide that during lent we are going to fast from any of these. These fasts end up with a different character than a fast from something we need. The act of refraining from them is an object lesson to ourselves that we don't need these things, whereas fasting from foods reminds us that normally we do, in fact need nutrients.

Fasting from certain attitudes is also an option. This is more difficult to measure. It is wise to be realistic and specific. For example, I would be unlikely to go forty days without being negative. If I set a plan to fast from negativity toward my children or spouse, I would be much more likely to achieve this goal... and to know if I did.

The bottom line is that the more difficult the fast is, the more often we think of and lean on God. These are good things to do. But the challenge is that this can easily lead to a gleeful sort of self-punishment that is not helpful. This sort-of punishment can feed into self-destructive messages and scripts that are not Godly at all.

EXCLUSIVE PREVIEW OF 'BUILDING YOUR SPIRITUAL PRACTICE'

If you are looking for more support in taking some next steps after these 40 days conclude, 'Building Your Spiritual Practice' by Jeff Campbell is one place to begin. A free preview of the introduction is presented here for your convenience.

Introduction

When somebody wants you to do something, it all boils down to a couple of simple questions:

Why should I do that?

How do I do that?

So, let's get straight to it. There is something I think you should do. I think you ought to have a spiritual practice. By this I mean that I think meditation and other contemplative activities ought to be a part of your life. I have a sense about one effective way to do this. I built my own spiritual practice and helped countless others do the same, through my website, *The Faith-ing Project,* dozens of email explorations, and a handful of books.

These practices lead to a way of living in the universe that changes everything. In some ways, it's analogous to living healthily. On one level, living healthily might be defined as doing the right exercises and eating the right foods. But of course, it's not really about the specific diet or exercise. Exercise and healthy eating are gateways that give us access to living longer and feeling better.

It's worth noticing that there are lots of healthy ways to eat. There are many effective physical fitness exercises. After a person learns a few basics, they are prepared to begin choosing meals and exercises that are best for them. It is not different when it comes to building a spiritual practice.

In this book, I will do my best to explain why a person ought to build a spiritual practice.

And I will do my best to explain how a person could build a spiritual practice.

This book is organized this is like a sandwich. The bread? That's the question of "why." I will address the question of "why" at both the beginning and the end of this book, much as a sandwich has bread at the top and the bottom. I will do this because the question of 'why' is a complicated one.

As a person builds her spiritual practice, she might, early on, answer that question in a certain way. The opening of this book will deliver some introductory answers to that question. It will hopefully deliver on some reasons to get this process started.

The bottom piece of bread will delve a little deeper. It will explore some answers to the question "why" that I personally would not have been able to come up with when I first started down this path. Some of these will be an explanation of who I am becoming and how I view the world. In some cases, it might be hard to see this stuff at all. I hope that by the time we get there, I have earned a little trust from you. It might be that you will take my word for it on some of these things.

(I will probably have lots of this stuff wrong by the way. I imagine if I wrote this book at some point further along in my journey, my ways of looking at the "why" will be quite different.)

Of course, a couple pieces of bread are boring without something to go between them. And it would be a bit of a tease if I shared with you why I think you ought to do a thing without explaining how it is that you ought to do it. So, in the middle of this book, you can expect to find an exploration of how you can build a spiritual practice.

This exploration will address some things that are relevant to nearly every kind of practice. It will also feature a brief exploration of several different spiritual exercises a person ought to consider. I don't think your spiritual practice should look exactly like my spiritual practice. It also shouldn't look like your neighbors, your spouses, or your parents.

I will do the best I can at exposing you to several different possibilities. But humanity has been at this for thousands of years. This book is a place to begin. It is the very first steps. I will offer you a few observations about where and how I think these practices might be effective. But mostly, you will learn what works for you by trying them out.

After you take these first couple steps, you might take a third and a fourth step with the other *Faith-ing Project* Guides or website. But this is still just the first few steps. I hope, sincerely, that you go deeper. There will be truths I fail to convey. There will be critical details I miss. As you begin to discover the practices that work for you, I hope that you will explore the rich and varied sources that inspired my attempts at portraying them here.

Before we go too much further let's spend a few minutes with some of the words that are likely to pop up along the way. These are words that are often used in these kinds of endeavors. It is probably helpful to understand a little something about how I am using them.

Let's begin with one of the more general terms: *contemplation* (and of course, all the related forms of the word like contemplative.) I was thrilled, recently, to discover that the term 'contemplation' is related to the word temple. It is obvious once it is pointed out. Most of the letters are sitting there, right in the middle of the word. The prefix, "con" means "with." On a basic level, then, "contemplation" is related to the way a person might look at the world from inside a temple. The wonderful thing is that the temple is already within us.

More specifically, I will use the word "contemplation" to refer to a broad category of ways of seeing the world, a way of progressing, a way of seeing. There are many ways to contemplate. Two that concern us here are *prayer* and *meditation.*

I will use the word "prayer" to mean certain types of contemplative activities which are connected to connection with something bigger than us. Prayer can be a kind of conversation. Most forms of prayer assume a divine listener. A spirit-entity we might (or might not) call God.

I will use the word "meditation." to mean certain types of contemplative activities which are less word dependent. Often, in meditation, there will be no assumption of a force above and beyond us.

In a book focused on these two things, it can grow monotonous to use the same 2 words repeatedly. As a result, I will sometimes use words like "spiritual exercise" or "practice." But the word "practice" is a little tricky. I will follow the conventions of language and use it sometimes to mean one specific set of things to do, a form of meditation and prayer. Other times, it has a wider meaning. A practice is also an ongoing commitment to do the best we can. A medical doctor or therapist might discuss their private practice. As a Special Education Teacher, I might refer to my practice, too. By this, I might mean the collection of all the things I do in my class to ensure that students are learning and being safe.

In a wider sense, then, when we discuss a Spiritual Practice, we mean something broader than one particular method of meditation or prayer. A spiritual practice in this broad sense is what the title of this book refers to. It is our ongoing promise to ourselves, our plan of which specific prayers and meditations we will engage in daily.

It is worth noting that reading this book is a bit like dipping a toe into the ocean. This is a vast and wonderful territory. There are some practices we will not explore at all because they are not the sort of things easily expressed in a book. Many of these are spiritual practice which help us to remember the body: dancing, yoga, drumming, and art for example.

There are other spiritual practices which are neither meditation nor prayer. Fasting, giving, and many forms of worship are also spiritual practices which I hope you will explore. But they will not be covered here, either.

In fact, even the practices we begin to explore here will only be introduced briefly. I hope that the brief introductions made here lead to a long-standing relationship. Practicing these every day will lead to a deeper relationship. So, will going to the source of these practices and exploring them in their spiritual context.

And so, if the time we spend together on this journey is short of long, I am thankful for your time and trust on this part of it. Let's begin with the question of why a person ought to build a spiritual practice at all.

The First Why

Let's look at some reasons we might want to build a spiritual practice.

Last chapter, I shared the idea that a spiritual practice is a regular commitment to meditating and praying. At this point, it's probably wise to take a closer look at this idea. It is all well and good to throw around those words. But it is worth wondering what this all means.

What that means is this: you should dedicate yourself to at least half an hour a day of doing nothing. I say that with my tongue only a little bit in my cheek.

In the west, we often throw around words like "meditation." These words have a sort of mystique about them. We can say them and feel a little bit of pride in ourselves. In the east, the words they sometimes use is the language's equivalent to simply "sitting." No big ideas or navel gazing. Just sitting.

This is not as easy as it sounds. There are lots of ways to do it. Some of these different ways of sitting lead to certain positive results. Others lead to other positive results. Some are good for nearly anybody. Others are good for only a certain type of person.

We will explore these different options soon enough. The bulk of this book will be a survey of several different types of meditation and prayer. But let's begin with a broad understanding of the goal. What we are talking about here is slowing down, releasing pretty much everything. Eventually, getting up to at least half an hour a day of it.

I am sure there are lots of things in your life that sound like they would be better to do than nothing. I am sure that the millions of different ways we entertain ourselves, the countless ways we want to be productive seem like much better choices than sitting.

This, then, brings us back to the "why." Why would we want to do nothing when there are so many good things we could be doing?

This discussion of the "why" is going to be rather abstract and theoretical if we don't root it in the actual practice of sitting. So, before we take a deeper look at the question of "why." I wonder if you might indulge me. Let's give our first practice a try before we proceed.

Practice #1: Simply Breathing

Preparation: This practice is very, very simple. But before we begin, I would like to ask you a question: How long could you comfortably sit and do nothing? Perhaps it is only a minute. Perhaps it is thirty. However long you choose, could you try and push yourself? Would it be possible to add just a few more minutes onto whatever total you just decided?

1. *Create a calming space., Set your phone to 'do not disturb.' Light a candle if you would like.*
2. *Place your feet flat on the floor. Sit in a manner that is upright but not uncomfortable.*
3. *Inhale, through the nose if possible.*
4. *Exhale through the mouth.*
5. *With the next inhale, give some attention to really filling up the lungs. Place your hand on the belly. Feel the movement outward of your hand.*
6. *Exhale, feeling the belly moving in toward the spine.*

7. Continue for the time you have allocated for this practice today.

Some final introductory thoughts of 'Why.'

I am of two minds about simplicity of practice. There is a way in which our mission is accomplished right here. With this simple 7-step series of instructions.

This practice accomplishes a tremendous number of things. One way that we might begin to explore the "why" of spiritual practice is to take a careful look at what we are accomplishing here. Perhaps the most important thing we are doing here—perhaps the most important "why" -- is that we are facing our fears and worries head on. We are no longer running.

Almost everything we do is part of a huge pattern of denial and fear. We have been taught explicitly and implicitly to keep moving. To run from the fears that are chasing us. To drown out the voices that are whispering to us. We fill up our schedules. We turn on the radio.

We are so very afraid of silence and stillness.

This is a surprising statement for many. But to anyone who wants to resist this reality, I have a very simple question: *If we are not afraid of silence and stillness, why is it so very difficult to sit quietly for any kind of length of time at all?*

The glory of facing our fears by sitting with them is just this: we suddenly realize that there is nothing they can ever do to us. In fact, it is the denial of our fears are dangerous. Some of our fears are things we can do nothing about, but our failure to face them is what makes them grow large in our hearts. Other worries are things we can do something about. But we can only act if we have stopped running long enough to identify just what they are.

Closely connected to this fear is the message that we must always be productive. By sitting, we (ironically) take a stand against this message. It is one thing to say, "I am more valuable than the things I produce." It is another to take a period to stop producing.

If this is hard for you, you might find some solace in the possibility that this is a win-win. Anecdotal reports, research, and wisdom from the world's spiritual tradition all agree: a time of rest is vitally important. There are many quotes from many directions which are variations on the theme "On a normal day, I meditate (or pray) for an hour. On the days when I know I am going to be really busy; I meditate (or pray) for two hours." At least one of the things meant by these quotes is this: when we take a moment to be non-productive, we end up more than compensating for the so-called lost productivity. When we return to our work, we end up being much more productive.

The final "why" we are going to consider for now is the quieting of the mind. Our brains produce a cacophony of noise. The job of this organ is to think. From a certain vantage point, it is very good at this.

There is a limit to the usefulness of our thoughts, though. Especially when we stand in the middle of too many of them. Like a wise man standing in a crowd, our best thoughts can get drowned out from the babble coming from all the others. There are many sorts of things our thoughts don't help us solve. There are some sorts of things that our thoughts in fact make worse.

There are many things in our minds which are difficult to notice when our thoughts are taking center stage. We have feelings, of course. These feelings are valuable guides as we become aware of them. Our mind is also where we become aware of bodily sensations. Sometimes this awareness is important on a sheerly physical level. We notice that our heel is sore, and we need new shoes. We note a growing pain in our belly which requires medical intervention. But more than this, the body has its own wisdom. When we turn down our thoughts, we tune into the things that the body is trying to tell us: the tension in our shoulders says, "don't trust this person." The quickening of our breath tells us that we were angry about something we aren't having an easy time of owning. It is easy to miss these signals when the babble of our brains is uncontested.

Those of us who believe in something greater than us—call it God for lack of a better, more inclusive term—are generally aware that God speaks in a still, quiet voice. It can be difficult to hear this voice sometimes. When our brain is busy over producing, it can be even more difficult to truly discern what is coming from us and what comes from elsewhere.

There are a few common misconceptions to clear up before we move from the "why" to the "what." The first common misconception is that the brain is bad and thoughts are not helpful.

Collectively and individually, we owe our brains and thoughts quite a lot. We could not be where we are without them. Our brain is like a hammer. Our thoughts are like nails. There are lots of things that hammers, and nails are good for. But a hammer and nails can't do everything. They can't turn screws. They can't saw boards in half. The situation we find ourselves in is as if we have gotten very good at hammering and have now begun to try to use the hammer to solve all our problems. It simply won't work.